(SheeMuAwn)

Broken and Poured Out:
A Korean's Journey with Jesus

Ki Dong Kim

with Jimi Miller

예수 그리스도는 어제나 오늘이나 영원토록
동일하시니라

Jesus Christ is the same yesterday, today and forever. Hebrews 13:8. NIV

Semone

(SheeMuAwn)

...the Lord reminded me that I was to carry only His burdens, and carry them in silence (page 88).

When their criticism against me turned into shouting even while I was preaching, branding me heretic and even sheep stealer, I renewed my decision to keep a pebble in my mouth as a reminder never to criticize...

"What's the matter with you?" some of the people demanded of me. "Why don't you answer them back? Why don't you shut them up? You see, but you don't talk!" And they gave me the nickname, "Semone" (the mute) (page 120).

 Unless otherwise identified, Scripture quotations are from the King James Version of the Bible. Scripture quotations marked NIV are taken from the HOLY BIBLE, NEW INTERNATIONAL VERSION®, copyright © 1973, 1978, 1984 by International Bible Society. Used by permission of Zondervan Publishing House.

To retain the foreign flavor of this material, the writer has not consistently conformed her style to our meticulous style guide.

Treasure House
An Imprint of
Destiny Image® Publishers, Inc.
P.O. Box 310
Shippensburg, PA 17257-0310

"For where your treasure is
there will your heart be also." Matthew 6:21

ISBN 1-56043-266-7
For Worldwide Distribution
Printed in the U.S.A.
Cover design by: Nikki Kobert

To My Wife...

With deep appreciation I know that if my wife, Kang Soon, a beautiful woman of prayer, had not married me, I would be in a totally helpless situation today. She is a most humble person, better than I.

KKD

Endorsements

Rarely does an autobiography rise above a focus on the self as does Ki Dong Kim's historical pilgrimage from the 1950's to the present. ***Semone*** *will both humble and inspire the reader...This is truly and blessedly a story of God's grace.*

Terry Lindvall, President
Regent University

How does a church congregation grow from 7 to 80,000 [adults] in 25 years? ...Here is a story that can shake the most ardent of Pentecostals and the most conservative of Presbyterians. Would God do for America what He is doing in Korea? My guess is yes, if we professing Christians would pay the same price.

Kenneth Taylor, Founder/President
Tyndale House Publishers

Contents

One

Hiding Place

"A bruised reed he will not break, and a smoldering wick he will not snuff out, till he leads justice to victory." Matthew 12:20 NIV

December 1957: Yesan, South Korea

By the fourth of my six days alone in fasting-prayer underneath the old First Methodist Church in Yesan, both ground and air are bitterly cold. I have been dozing fitfully, dreaming weird dreams that warn me I am nearing literal starvation. It is time to go; I must find food somewhere. But for a moment longer, I lie still listening to the dead silence.

Mustering a spurt of energy, I push myself up on my hands and knees and crawl in the dirt back toward the ragged hole in the ceiling over my head–actually, the underside of the church floor–my one and only way out of the crawlspace. With no trace of light filtering down, I cannot locate the hole. I move my hands around in the dark up under the splintery wood, and finally discover the hole. But it is blocked, covered over by some large, solid object that I cannot budge. I am trapped.

Frantic and confused, I crawl back to my place and collapse shivering onto my straw mat, the only protection separating the thin rags covering my body from the frost-hardened earth. My teeth chatter as the tormenting theme of recurring nightmares closes in upon me: In them I see my distraught Christian friends discover my frozen corpse under the church floor. I watch them roll my stiffened body up in my ragged mat, then drag it out and away to the burial place, and I watch them bury me in the ground. That's how I know that I will die; I am just not sure when or how long it will take.

On my sixth day without food or water, I lie motionless, noticing with slight interest that there is no more pain in my body, no more itch, no more ache. My feet, covered only by brittle strands of woven dry grass, are no longer cold. I am glad not to feel anything. Willing myself to be with Christ and out of my misery, I feel peace. At the same time, even though I have never been religious, confusing thought patterns of Korea's national religions war with my growing knowledge of God's Word (along with my gross ignorance of His ways), and I lie there thinking, *At last I am dead, and I did not have to do it to myself. My body and the hopeless human person inside my body are dead, and I am glad. Maybe I will come back reincarnated, as the Buddhists believe, in a lower life-form like an ox or maybe as a dog–some family's pet–and they will feed me, and I won't starve anymore.*

I open my eyes a slit. I see brief puffs of breath blowing cloudy-white from my nostrils into the bitter stillness, and with a pang of disappointment realize that I am still alive. I focus my eyes on a ragged, dusty cobweb, hanging limp and lifeless, and think, *Just like me. No hope for me.* I shiver. Feeling comes back into my body, the grueling despair, and memories: *My little sister lies dying from the shrapnel of a bomb and I clean and shine shoes for money to buy her a little rice cake and bring it home too late! too late! and I throw the cake and shoe-shine box into the creek far away, far far away from me.*

I cannot remember if I took the quinine pills (popular pills for suicide in Korea). I only remember settling down and thinking how cold I am, weak and aching all over from the perpetual misery of malnutrition.

But then, without regret I remember the past seventy wonder-filled days since I gave my heart to Jesus. All during those days I have been saturating my mind and imagination with the astonishing words in God's Holy Bible, in the ten different Bibles I borrowed from the Presbyterians, reading each one front to back, cover to cover, one after the other. I cannot get enough of God's Word. I devour the meat of it like a starving wolf. With all my heart, I want to serve Jesus, and now some of God's words come to my mind:

> [You] *are dead, and your life is hid with Christ in God* (Colossians 3:3).

Without hope of a future in this world, I lie still, pondering those words, trying to make them happen, trying to surrender my life up to God, but suddenly I cry out in anguish, "No! How can I leave my family? How can I abandon them? Who will feed them? I alone feed them! With all this total responsibility for them, how have I come to be in this hopeless situation?"

Then I remember: Earlier in the month, when it came time to clean up at the church in honor of the approaching Christmas season, the other young men worked together outside cleaning the windows and yard, but I went inside to clean somewhere alone. I was too ashamed of my stutter, my tattered army fatigues, and my lack of family status to present myself as one of them. In the remotest corner of the sanctuary where no one else would clean, I discovered the hole broken through the old wooden floor into the darkness below. I wondered what was down there. The hole opened just wide enough for my skin and bones to shimmy through without space to spare, and shimmy down through I did. As my eyes adjusted to the eerie light under the low church floor, I burrowed to a place high enough for me to stand up. *Ah,* I thought, *this place is cold, but it is my place!* I cleared away mouse dung and cobwebs and claimed that dark and secluded place as my refuge. And when I went home, I held that secret place in my heart. A week later, when I became seventy days old as a newborn Christian, I crawled down into that place to hide from everyone except my Lord and Savior, to celebrate my first Christmas alone with Him in fasting-prayer for six days. And that's how I came to be trapped under the church.

Whenever I spoke in public, my words would hammer out like a woodpecker tapping on a tree. But whenever I am alone with God, my words flow like a mountain stream, and this time I prayed aloud, "O Lord, I want to serve You; I want to be a fisher of men for You, like Pastor Kyung Lin Oh, but I am so shy, so worthless, so poor, so uneducated, You cannot use me. But I want to be used. O God, I am a failure, a bad person. You know my heart, that I want to die and be with You, to serve You in Your presence, to be rid of this life of misery and poverty and all the sickness and all the killing."

I had brought neither food nor water, but as always I had quinine pills with me, thirty of them wrapped tightly into a small package. A spirit of suicide hovered over our impoverished nation at war with itself, and the demon that drove me even as a Christian was the nagging temptation to swallow all thirty pills at one time.

Suddenly, I wonder, *Have I already taken them?* I cannot remember. It doesn't matter. I am already dying. But then, from a distance I hear a muffled cacophony of voices growing louder, louder. A thrill of fear sweeps through every nerve in my body: Who? Communist soldiers? No, this is 1957. The Korean War has been officially over for almost five years. Under the United Nations occupation, peace reigns in South Korea.

Who then? God's angels? Or men calling me back to life?

Heavy footsteps on the floor over my head shower ancient wood dust into my face, and a sudden bright blade of light slices down through a crack between the floorboards. Then I know: In the sanctuary directly over my head Pastor Oh has called the pre-dawn worshipers to prayer.

With a surge of energy, I leap to my feet, and hammer under the floor bruising my fists, sinking wood splinters into my flesh. I cry out for help. But the chorus of loud, uninhibited voices from the worshipers overhead smothers all the noise I can make.

I search for a loose-hanging board to pound under the floor, but there is none. Frantically, I scratch in the dirt for something, anything I can use to draw someone's attention before they all leave for the day. Nothing, except one brittle scrap of paper. With my last vestige of strength, I crawl to the gash of light. With fingers stiff from cold, I stuff the paper up through the crack and wriggle it around and around, back and forth, praying to God that someone will see it and save me.

Two

Runaway

Behold, the eye of the Lord is upon them…to deliver their soul from death, and to keep them alive in famine. Psalm 33:18,19

December 1957, June 1938–1952: Yesan, Seosan, Hongsung, Yesan

Above my head, unseen by me, my beloved Pastor Oh stands behind his pulpit, shouting praises and petitions to God with all his might, when suddenly from the corner of his eye he sees an odd movement near his right foot—a scrap of paper apparently trying to wriggle up between the floorboards.

From underneath, I watch the paper disappear. I hold my breath as the voices become quiet. What is happening? Overhead, the floor vibrates with the stamping of many feet followed by a rumble like thunder, and a circle of dim light penetrates my darkness through the hole that had been covered over by a heavy pedal-organ. I scramble to the light, towards a sea of smiling faces peering down at me, and I see the hand of Pastor Oh reaching down to grasp mine. With great difficulty, this rescued, humiliated, pitiful poorest-of-the-poor crawls up from under the church–a nineteen-year-old starving child of God.

I am Kim, Ki Dong. Kim is my family name; Ki Dong, my person in the Kim clan. I am also known as Ki Dong Kim–same name, Western style.

On June 25, 1938, twenty-eight years after Japan's imperious annexation of the entire peninsula of Korea, the Land of Morning Calm, I was born the second son, fifth child of eight, to our father Kim, Jung Han and our mother Jung, Young-E, into their divested remnant of a formerly wealthy *yangban* clan of Korean aristocrats.

In the late 19th century, two major historical events occurred in Korea that changed the direction of our national life and politics:

The first occurred in 1884, when Protestant Christianity was introduced by Dr. Horace N. Allen, an American medical missionary. Dr. Allen was soon followed by others from Canada, England, and the United States–stalwarts who came to us, "people walking in darkness...living in the land of the shadow of death..." (Is. 9:2 NIV). Despite threats of torture and death, they shined the light of the Gospel of Jesus Christ into our darkness, and the darkness was unable to snuff it out (Jn. 1:5). Given permission by the government to build mission schools, clinics and hospitals, but forbidden to proselytize, those tenacious light-bearers graciously taught our farmers a little something about modern agriculture, while gradually establishing denominational footholds. By teaching us Christian hymns and songs, they planted seeds of the Gospel of Jesus Christ deep into the soil of many weary hearts.

The second major event, which in effect deposed Korea's upper and ruling classes, was Japan's collusion on October 8, 1895, with the assassins of our conservative, pro-Chinese Queen Min. This collusion opened the nation to Japan's political control for fifteen years followed by formal annexation of the entire peninsula into the Japanese empire, confiscation of all our farming lands, and the enactment of arbitrary laws compelling us to substitute Japanese names for our family names, and to worship the Japanese emperor as god. With guns to heads, on September 9, 1938, a few splintered church groups took an "Intra-denominational Conference vote" publicly, and agreed to comply. They survived. Those who refused, disappeared from view.

Meanwhile, my clan, the proud yangban Kim, were above all that; they acknowledged no idols, believed in no gods, and accredited only themselves. They simply accepted all the local religions as undeniable aspects of our national culture, but worship was not for them. Robbed of their wealth and with no religious convictions to sustain them, when family status dissolved, they were left with nothing upon which to stand firm.

Even though one of our close relatives was General Kim, Chwah Jin, a famous Korean warrior who caused much grief to the Japanese during the Ch'ongsan-ri battle, my immediate family was reduced to living in a common house on a hill at the end of a two-rut road in the poor village of Seosan at the foot of Hung Mountain in South Choongnam Province. By the time of my birth, Korea was a somber, demonized nation with little knowledge of God, in "great distress with perplexity" (Lk. 21:25), suffocating beneath a blanket of hopelessness, superstition and religious confusion:

Confucianism, for example, instructed us to be polite to dead persons, to be kind to each other, and to show respect first to the king, then to the father, and so on down the line, but offered no hope of a future.

Animism induced in us fear of every rock and tree, and offered no hope.

Buddhism taught us to behave or else be reincarnated as a lower life-form, while demanding servile bondage to aimlessly wandering spirits of the dead seeking nothingness.

Shamanism required homage to demons as friends who would bring us good luck, and who needed to be offered rice when we were either dining at the table, or burning incense to dead ancestors.

All our villages, towns, and even the very land itself lay stifled under a cloak of subjection, rejection, failure and shame.

Not only that, but our foreign overlords threatened dire punishment for any Koreans who spoke, wrote, or published in our native tongue, or taught their children the history or traditions of our forefathers, even in the privacy of their homes.

At the same time, the robbed and deposed, angry and autocratic yangban parents stubbornly refused to bend their backs or dirty their hands with hard labor even to improve their own or their children's deplorable living conditions. Consequently, they expended most of their energy in loud arguments and fights among themselves. But even while deep depression clouded hearts, minds and imaginations, Korea's unconquerable spirit awaited her time to rise from the dust.

I was seven years old in 1945, when America's atomic bombs fell on the cities of Nagasaki and Hiroshima in Japan, thereby ending World War II in the Pacific. Our defeated Japanese colonizers were then expelled from all of Korea by Russian troops moving down from the north and by American forces coming up from the south. The Allies brought peace to Korea, restoring our land and family names, our alphabet and language, and our presses ran again. And even as the Allies arbitrarily split us apart at the 38th parallel, our divided people throbbed with the hope of future reunification into one sovereign and independent nation. And, for the next two years, South Korea saw hope of prosperity under the benevolent administration of our elected President Syngman Rhee, who established freedom of religion and the press.

Events that occurred in the year 1948 brought understandable confusion to my ten-year-old mind. I was living at home in Seosan when my grandmother on my mother's side, our only still-wealthy relative, donated her remaining small fortune to the building of a Buddhist temple, despite having never practiced Buddhism herself. In doing this she left the rest of the clan destitute and without hope of any help from her. She died soon thereafter, followed closely by eleven members of her immediate family, who all died miserably as if under a curse.

That same year, our family moved. In his youth, my father had little access to schooling or modern learning for himself. Now he wanted to enable his children to receive at least an elementary school education. Since there was no school in Seosan, he moved our family to Hongsung near Gal Mountain, where we had relatives. He could afford to rent only one room for the ten of us, but at least now his children could attend school.

I soon discovered that I loved learning. In early 1950, at the beginning of my sixth year in school, the refugee government held a nationwide examination for over 400 potential graduates from elementary school. I was graded thirty-eighth from the top and accepted as an honor student. That meant there was hope for me—hope of realizing my dreams of an education and a future materializing out of our despair and poverty, hope that someday my family would have good clothes and regular meals. At that time, even my elder brother, a high official of the government-owned South Korea Railroad, was unable to help us. His pay was so meager, he could hardly afford to feed his own family. But my hope for a brighter future was short-lived.

On my twelfth birthday, June 25, 1950, less than a year after the American occupying forces returned home to the United States, to our horror and dismay, troops from Communist North Korea invaded South Korea in a sudden, bloody frenzy, overwhelming our capital city of Seoul within two days.

War was declared. Many of our cousin-brothers (the males in our extended family) went to war against each other, and tragic reports filtered down to us: This cousin was killed over here, that one over there; another one died of his wounds, probably from neglect, or more probably from infections caused by the traditional Korean medical treatment of wounds using poultices of cow dung and herbs.

The United Nations quickly and officially condemned the invasion by the North as a violation of international peace, but the Communists kept coming. Supplied with arms and ammunition by both China and Russia, they slaughtered our people, destroyed our forests, and devastated our land. When the routed South Korean government retreated south from Seoul, my elder brother fled with them.

With Communist soldiers occupying our village of Hongsung, I had to go high in the mountains to gather wood. Brokenhearted, I often stayed there all day crying, shedding copious tears of sorrow and despair. What would become of us? I had no way of knowing that there was a loving God in heaven watching me, Whose heart was also breaking.

Soon my father faced the inevitable: The only way he could feed his large family was to help prepare food for the occupying enemy troops. That way, after they ate, he could collect any remaining rice and bring it home to us. But when the North Koreans learned that my elder brother was a high official of the South Korea Government Railroad, they imprisoned our father and beat him without mercy, disabling his body and destroying his health.

Meanwhile, the displaced South Korean Army, bolstered by arms and support from sixteen member-nations of the United Nations, rallied, regrouped, and soon reoccupied our small town. Within two months of the initial overthrow of Seoul, our men recaptured that city also, and the invaders fled north. The Allies followed. In less than a month, they captured Pyongyang, the capital of North Korea. But when the Chinese soldiers joined North Korea in the battle, the Allies again retreated south. In January 1951, the Communists again occupied Seoul, and again retreated in March, when the Allies reoccupied the city. So it went back and forth. We were never sure where the line separating North from South was drawn.

Meanwhile, when our own soldiers learned that our crippled father had helped to feed the enemy, he became a traitor in their eyes. They too arrested him and beat him until he was the same as dead. Many desperate fathers like mine, who did what little they could to help their families survive, were convicted without a trial. Some were summarily shot; others, killed with a bamboo spear. Fortunately, my elder brother returned in the nick of time armed with an official pardon from Lee, Sung Mohn, and his own medal for bravery and loyalty to the South Korean government, bestowed by General Park himself, and thereby gained our father's freedom.

He was almost too late. By that time, our father could no longer even move by himself. After he was carried up the hill to his home, he lay on his mat on the floor all day and all night, striving with all his feeble strength to manage the family affairs from there. Consequently, at the awkward age of twelve, I had to work somewhere at something so the rest of our family could survive, at least until...

Until what? The war continued to rage all around us, and no one knew what to expect from the bleak and dismal future.

In the spring of 1951, when I was not quite thirteen, my disabled father somehow managed with futile promises to borrow a certain amount of barley from a neighbor for us to eat and to plant. But our crop failed. At the end of the year, when it was time for him to repay double the amount, as was the Korean custom at the time, there was no possible way. The responsibility then fell to me, the oldest boy in the home, to work off the debt as a servant for that neighboring family for an entire year to recompense them for the barley we had already eaten. Every morning thereafter I got up very early. After chores at home, I hauled twigs and branches down from the ravaged mountain forest to the neighbors' house, fed their cows, carried their water from the well, and made their cooking fire inside and another fire in the outdoor fire-pit, which sent warm smoke flowing through the hollow shaft under their *ondul* floors to heat the house. It was hard, hard labor, but in this way I could serve my family.

During that time, on every fifth day, our mother carried her rice-straw basket about twenty miles to the town market and purchased seaweed, fish, and other items for our neighbors who were too busy to go for themselves. With her full basket balanced on her head, she returned home and bartered with the villagers for their crops, chickens, or whatever else they had that she needed for our family.

Before long, the neighbors I worked for saw that I was a good, hard worker, and offered to pay me with lots of wonderful rice to feed my family in order to keep me working for them. (The wealthy ate rice; the poor like us ate barley.)

About that same time, an aunt offered me a parcel of land she owned if I would work for her for several years. Both offers were great temptations; either way I could earn enough to continue feeding my destitute family. But my deep desire—the burning desire of my heart—was to study and to learn. And, because of my debilitating stutter, I wanted to study alone.

I continued to work for the neighbor family, slowly paying off the debt, until the school in Hongsung was forced to close down. I then faced a severe crisis in having to choose between two options: to serve as somebody's house servant possibly for the rest of my life; or, to leave my starving family, my poor father sick and near death, and my tired mother overworked with little to show for it, and run away to school somewhere.

In 1952, even in the throes of war, the South Korean government tried to maintain some semblance of normalcy by keeping at least some schools open, and I heard that the new term at the middle school in Yesan would start in April. But Yesan was fifteen miles away from Hongsung on the other side of the mountain. Still, I longed to go even though I had little reason to hope for encouragement from anyone. Besides being dirt poor, I was extremely nervous in front of others, fearful of trying to speak to anyone, flat-footed in both feet, and had a face burned black by the sun, with the hard, pinched look of poverty. But I also had a reputation in the town: Everybody knew who I was, the withdrawn boy who feeds his family. On the street, even the mayor of Hongsung recognized me, the destitute boy with the strong will.

The very day I finally satisfied our debt to the neighbor, I made an agonizing decision: *I will go to the principal of the school in Yesan and work for him. He will give me the chance to study, and I will still send food home to my family.*

I had no reason to believe this was so, no guarantee that I would even be able to fill my own mouth and stomach, except that I willed to work hard enough to make it happen. Every aspect of my upbringing, however, argued against this plan: According to Korean tradition, I had no right to leave my father. Dishonoring the father by deserting him, the Korean son forfeits his own identity and becomes a nobody. In my heart, I knew leaving my father would be like cutting off my arm. If I failed to succeed, I could never return home. Besides, I had no idea how to find Yesan beyond the bombed-out, mountainous landscape of stumps and broken trees.

But the spring term would begin any day; so, as soon as darkness fell, I stood outdoors in our yard in the pouring rain, in my patched, knee-length, gray-beige rags that were soaked through to my skin, and my braided-grass sandals already heavy with mud. I was fully aware of dangers everywhere: wartime killing daily on the streets even in broad daylight; hundreds of our townspeople senselessly slaughtered by the enemy; starving and confused strangers and neighbors with sharpened bamboo spears, prowling the woods at night in their search for food, ready to attack any other living thing that moved.

With nothing in my hands, I stood alone in the yard by the outside entrance to the house. Hidden by the absolute darkness of the downpour where I could safely cry, I shouted silently deep within my heart, *To live I must learn! To live I must learn! Education for me is the only way for my family to survive!*

Back and forth, back and forth I stalked, fell in the mud, dragged myself back up onto my feet, all the while feeling the rain wash the flood of bitter tears from my face. I could not tear my eyes away from the house. Father would never know the pain that pierced me through. Finally, I faced the bitter, cold reality: I had to go. There was no other way.

With my heart exploding inside my body, I turned towards the room where my father lay and kneeled down in the muck. With my face almost in the mud, I made a low formal bow of respect towards my poor father asleep inside. With my voice I cried out as I pictured the faces of my crippled father, my exhausted mother, my hungry brothers and sisters. Then swiftly, abruptly I stood, turned away from my father's house, and half-blinded by tears took off running down the war-desecrated hill alongside the newly-turned muddy road.

Three

Just This Once

He...sat down...and prayed that he might die. "I have had enough, Lord," he said. "Take my life; I am no better than my ancestors."

1 Kings 19:4 NIV

1952–1957: Yesan

Trusting neither the earth beneath my feet nor any other living thing, I ran all night through the pounding rain, dodging as best I could the snatching underbrush and the real and imagined terrors of the lightless, treeless, steep-sloped mountain that had once been a forest. I flinched at every sound, every snapping twig that might signal one of the fifty or so check points where friend or enemy—there was no way to distinguish—would stop and question and maybe kill me on the spot: soldiers or civilians, terrified people trying to find food, running away from each other, not knowing who is who, afraid of the night, afraid of the dead, but more afraid of the living. With no known border between North and South, all was confusion.

Weeping blindly, I concentrated on each step pulling me forward, steeled against whatever real or surreal evil might overtake me from behind.

When dawn finally crawled over the mountain, I was amazed to still be alive, standing on a muddy, cobbled street in the center of old Yesan, surrounded by the war's torched and trampled fields. Any new rips and tears in my clothes or cuts in my skin, any new bruises and bloody wounds under the thick dirt on my feet were of no concern to me. I had made it to Yesan.

As soon as I arrived at a rambling house, which I assumed belonged to the school principal, I stopped in amazement to survey my surroundings through tired and bloodshot eyes. The house in front of me stood in stark contrast to the many thickly-thatched, humped-roofed, low, common houses. Its roof stood out grandly, a high roof of black tile with gaily lifting corners that presumed to bar evil spirits from plopping down into the yard to harass and tease the inhabitants. To me the house seemed like a palace. Such houses were rare in those villages. In my limited experience, a black-tile roof designated a well-to-do, aristocratic family.

I guessed correctly that it was the principal's home. No doubt the appearance of one such as I, dressed in filthy, rain-drenched rags, with scraggly pig-tailed head and bleeding feet, seemed strangely out of place to the servants moving around inside who peered through the lattices at the skinny beggar just down from the mountain.

I noticed that the principal's plowed garden had not yet been planted: No cabbage or even radish sprouts peeked up from the orderly rows. Brown-clay storage jars, big enough to crawl into, lay on their sides empty, which suggested to me that the family might need another worker.

I thought, *Well, the way to go into the working place is to start working. Nobody likes to clean the dirtiest place, so that is my job. I have to start from that place. I am not too good or too important to start at the bottom.*

Without saying anything to anyone, I crossed into the back yard, followed the familiar stench to the filthy toilet house, and started cleaning. First, I scooped all the dirt out of the two enormous ceramic toilet bowls and dumped it into the buckets. Then, like a Chinese coolie, I carried the full buckets suspended from a pole across my shoulders out to the garden. I adopted that as my job.

From inside the house the principal, his wife, their four children, and the servants all watched me working very hard for them outside. When the principal called me to the kitchen door, I was so embarrassed by my dirty hands and hair and ragged clothes, that I stuttered like a croaking toad.

But the principal was patient and kind, and very generous. He encouraged me to clean myself up at the village water pump, and then come into the house and eat rice with them. I could hardly believe it: Rice! Ah, from then on, my vision of going back to school sometime in the future grew brighter every day.

Eventually, the family gave me clothes and took me in as their house servant. Within several months, I was working two other positions as well, as an office servant during the day, and as a mechanic at night.

On July 27, 1953, a truce agreement was signed by the United Nations and North Korea, and the fighting ended. As hundreds of thousands of North Korean refugees flooded down into South Korea seeking asylum, our local leaders in Yesan opened an evening school for them in army tents; and although my very tight work schedule made it impossible for me to attend day school, I was able to enroll in that evening school.

Somehow I was elected president of the student body and given authority to tell the other students when to stand up, sit down, come here, go there, do this, do that. While I enjoyed feeling like the "king," bossing them around every day, in all other conversations I still stumbled over my tongue with the stutter I could not conquer.

In late 1954, my father died. Had he known that I attended school? Did he approve? I did not know. I was not yet sixteen years old, but following his death, the full care of the entire family fell to me as the oldest unmarried son. Together our family accompanied our father's coffin along the narrow mountain trail through the Valley of Sorrow to the cemetery. After we buried him, we all sat down and sobbed and cried. There was no comfort, no hope, no knowing what to do. We did not even know where the family should go, since they would soon have to leave the house where they had lived for so long. Had we owned even half an acre of land to farm, they could have stayed there in Hongsung.

I soon realized that, for them to survive, I had to move all of them up to Yesan, where I could at least keep them together, clothe and feed them. And so, leaving them behind temporarily, I returned to Yesan, rented one room with one tiny window in a small house near the principal's house, then went back down to Hongsung, and brought the first four members of my family back up with me. We lived together for awhile in that one room separated from the landlord only by a latchless, sliding, rice-paper door. After about a year, we moved into two rooms in another house as I added two more family members, then two more, until finally, twelve members of my extended family not including myself were living together: my widowed mother, her three widowed sisters, my two younger brothers, other cousin-brothers and sisters, and a nephew–twelve of them in two small rooms, each one traumatized into apathy and hollow silence. I did not allow them to quarrel among themselves because I did not know how far they would go with it. Right away I established that I was "king" there. For their own survival they had to obey me.

Pumpkin was the cheapest vegetable to buy, so almost every day the women sliced up a pumpkin and boiled it to make soup, occasionally flavoring it with anchovies or some small herring or azaleas or chrysanthemums. They shared it together, eating just enough to fill their stomachs. Sadly, I watched them eating their poor portions, wishing they at least had the energy and the ingredients to make *kimchee* (Korea's main staple, similar to sauerkraut), soy sauce, or bean curd.

Each person had only the clothes on his or her back, faded gray or black-dyed, olive-drab army fatigues that were for sale cheap in every marketplace. No matter how tattered or torn they were, I could not foresee buying new clothes for any of us in the near future. We had no storage chest, no low tables, no cushions, no anything except tin bowls like beggars' bowls, one for each of them, which they carried with them, and their straw mats to sleep on. None of them worked because there were no jobs open to them. Even if there had been, they were all too depressed to concentrate on working at any job.

I was the only one who did anything. Whenever I insisted, one or the other would stumble up into the mountainside in search of roots or wild fresh greens for food. But the rest of the time, they stayed inside the house staring at the floor and the walls and each other's backs. They never talked. We had too many tragedies in our family for conversation: Our father dead from the torture, cousin-brothers killed in the wars, others dying from untreated diseases. With so much inner pain they had nothing to talk about with each other. They lived at the bottom of life, a hopeless situation. They were without hope, and hope continually frustrated makes the heart sick (Prov. 13:12a). They were of all people sick at heart. It was a miracle any of us survived.

I continued to work long, hard hours every day through three years of school plus one extra year to earn a diploma. By that time, the evening classes that met in session for thirty hours a week had moved from the army tents into deserted barracks, and a fee was being charged to all students in the sixth grade and beyond.

To me school was wonderful—we studied everything: language arts including poetry, arithmetic, social studies, nature classes, physical education including self-defense skills, practical arts, moral education, music, fine arts including calligraphy, folk dances and patriotic songs, drama and puppetry. The girls also learned flower arranging. We had mounds of homework every night.

Eventually, I advanced into high school where there were strict rules that all students must wear the official uniforms, lightweight for summer and heavy wool for winter, and keep their hair neatly cut, or else suffer punishment. But it was impossible for me to purchase any uniform, certainly not two. When the school principal gave me his daughter's old one, I simply converted it into a man's uniform by sewing the buttons to the other side. But it was old. When it began to wear out, the school board members made an exception to the uniform rule in my case, treating me as a special scholarship student. They allowed me to attend classes in my work clothes, not because I studied well, but because they knew I worked very hard to feed my family.

Even so, a cloud of gloom and dark despair was my constant companion during those high-school years after my father's death. I ate hardly anything. Sometimes, when I had a little money, I would buy noodles, cook them for myself, and eat. When I had no money, I did not eat. I missed a lot of meals in between. After doing that throughout most of 1955, my health began to fail from exhaustion and malnutrition. I became progressively weaker and forgetful. My vision began to fail. Friends and schoolmates were annoyed when I failed to greet them, but I could hardly distinguish faces and could not remember names. I had contracted the disease that had already killed three of my cousins, all but three of my cousin-brothers, and countless others nationwide—a disease of the liver, a plague that the doctors eventually attributed to our eating vegetables fertilized with human waste.

When the principal noticed that my skin and the whites of my eyes had turned bright yellow, he himself rushed me to the hospital. After the doctor checked my urine, which was dark gold in color, I overheard him talking behind the curtain. "This case of yellow jaundice (hepatitis) is not just serious," he said. "It's fatal. I am amazed that he is still alive. There is no hope for him." And he withheld medication from me in favor of those patients with some hope of recovery.

But someone at that hospital told me the one thing he had heard about Jesus Christ—that He is God. At the time, I denied any interest, but I could not forget the Name. After that person was gone, I thought about his words. The more I meditated on them, the more I started moving my head and my limbs, and stretching my muscles. After ten days of lying in the hospital bed with no medication and very little care, I sat up. Still very sick, I could at least walk, and I walked right out of the hospital.

As I left, the medical staff stared at me in wonder: How could anyone who was supposed to die, who still looked so much like the walking dead, get up and walk out the door?

Soon after, an old man gave me some medicine, a brew of herbs so bitter that it made my eyes water. He assured me it would heal my eyes and cure my liver disease. "If you want to live," he said, "you have to drink it all day from morning to night and in between. Pluck it for yourself, boil it and drink it instead of any other drink." For three months, I did as he said, crying all day long as I drank the bitter potion. After that my eyes began to focus normally, and I became fully alive once again.

After my complete recovery, I went to visit my uncle, my mother's brother, the self-appointed family scold. Whenever he saw me, he would approach all my problems from his authoritarian, yangban attitude, while intending to give me encouragement to show he cared what was happening to me. Along with a scolding on every subject imaginable, one question he kept throwing at me finally hit home: "Who are you? Who do you think you are?"

Later that same day, on my way home on the train, the same rhetorical question kept being thrown at me. Whenever someone bumped up against me, he would try to start an argument by demanding, "Who are you?"

No one really wanted an answer, but asking that sharp-edged question for the purpose of picking a fight was the day's popular way of speaking. People at that time were very poor, very stingy, annoyed with everything, always looking to brawl among themselves, trying to prove something. Accidently touch someone, and that person would respond, "Who are you?" We were still a nation at war, specifically within ourselves and with each other, suffering a national identity crisis.

At the end of the train ride, I changed to the bus, and again the same thing happened. I barely brushed up against somebody, and he growled at me: "Who are you? What kind of person are you?" Even though we all heard the same thing over and over, on that particular day, when so many people kept demanding that of me, it became my personal problem because I did not know the answer to the question: *Who am I?*

Throughout an entire week, I suffered from rehearsing that question over and over in my mind. One thing I did know, that my situation was altogether desperate: I had twelve mouths to feed besides my own, but no money, no abilities, no one to help me, no one else to take any of the pressure off of me even for a moment. No hope. I did not know who I was, and could foresee only one possible resolution to that dilemma.

All through that week, I reasoned thus: *When I was small boy, old uncle in long white robe with white fan, with hair coiled into top-knot under black horsehair hat tied under chin with ribbon, came with recognized authority from honorable yangban family background. He sat; we bowed very low to him, with eyes fixed on floor, waiting respectfully for him to speak. My father was yangban Kim, came down line from twenty-eight prime ministers. Before Japanese occupation and war, yangban have strongest family background, but now does not have many family members because enemies killed them. So, who are the Kim now? Who am I? Everybody asks me, but nobody knows. I give up. I am nobody. Solution: The only way out of this insolvable dilemma is death. I will kill myself, then I won't wonder about the answer to that unanswerable question anymore.*

Once I gave up, I experienced such amazing peace of mind that I went ahead and prepared for my suicide, politely visiting all the people I wanted to see for the last time, while amassing quinine pills, Korea's most popular pill at that time for that same purpose. As soon as I had thirty wrapped into one neat little package tucked deep down into my jacket pocket, the thought entered my mind, *Well, if there is God, maybe He knows who I am. Just once before I die, I will go to church and, if He is there, I will ask Him.*

Four

First Summons: Final Hope

"...This man is my chosen instrument...I will show him how much he must suffer for my name." Acts 9:15a,16 NIV

October–December 1957: Yesan

I had never before been inside any church building—had never even been invited into one except by a Roman Catholic priest. But his religion was too mystical for me, too much like Buddhist temple worship with candles and costumes, statues and incense and prayer beads.

Early on Sunday morning, October 18, 1957, from half a mile away I heard the deep, resounding bong-bong-bong of the ancient cast-iron bell summoning children to Sunday school at the old First Methodist Church of Yesan. I had once observed the bell's repercussions shaking the church's faded, red paint chips loose, and weakening its rusting roof. But in my twenty years, I had never once considered entering the crumbling, wooden building that had stood there for half a century. And I intentionally avoided the much newer, red brick Presbyterian church with the arched windows and tin roof that stood about 100 yards from our house, erected by and for North Korean refugees.

But on that particular Sunday when I heard the Methodist church bells, I thought, *I have to go to that church at least this one time. If there is God, I have to ask Him this question that I cannot answer, that I'm always asking myself: Who am I? If He knows, I then have to ask Him why my life is so desperate and so sad.*

Ashamed to present myself in public, I went down the unpaved road two hours early and hung around the crumbling original building in the churchyard while inspecting the new and unfinished, stone construction on the property in front of it. Completed from the ground up to only about five feet, the new structure had wooden window frames already darkened with dust.

When the adults started coming down the puddled, dirt roads towards the church, I turned my back for fear of being mocked, then I grabbed a straw broom and swept the entire sandy churchyard free of leaves and pebbles. After the children's Sunday school hour was over, it was time for the adult worship service to begin. But even after the adults left their dusty and muddy shoes at the door before entering the old building, no teacher invited me in.

Regardless, I stayed. I had no prior knowledge of the Bible, no knowledge of Jesus except that His name had been spoken to me that one time in the hospital. I stayed because I knew if I went home, I would never come back.

After all the other adults were inside, Pastor Kyung Lin Oh stood waiting outside at the door, watching me. I made a formal bow to him, left my muddy sandals next to several hundred other pairs, and followed him into the drafty building to a place on the front wooden bench on the men's side of the sanctuary.

Altogether, about 300 Christians had gathered there. When they all prayed out loud together, I had no idea what was going on. But after their prayer, I listened to the sermon–my very first sermon–about Jesus, Who said to some men, "Come, follow me...and I will make you fishers of men" (Mk. 1:17 NIV).

By the end of the service, I remembered only those three words, "fishers of men," because I had sat there watching Pastor Kyung Lin Oh, so merciful and benevolent, and thinking, *I want to be like you someday–a fisher of men.*

I went home and announced to my entire family that we were going to the Christian church together that night. The ones who came with me–my mother and my two younger brothers–all responded to the evening message and were miraculously converted that same night. The next morning, Monday, the four of us also attended the daily 4 a.m. prayer meeting.

That Monday was also the first day of a week of crusade-meetings at the Presbyterian church. Determined to learn all I could about the Christian religion no matter where I had to go to hear it–even there–I went, and at the very first meeting I was introduced to the shattering reality of sin.

I had never before heard of sin. But as I sat on the men's side of the big room, this time with over 350 other people, I listened to Hyung Tae Kim, the dynamic crusade leader from Sam-Kahk Mountain, the short-short man in the dark-dark blue suit, preach on our sin against man and against a holy God, and our desperate need for repentance and forgiveness. His message was so powerful, I was overcome with my guilt as a lost sinner. Suddenly, he pointed at me and said, "You, young man, how long have you been a Christian?"

Every eye looked in my direction. Mortified at being the center of attention, I told him, "Y-y-yesterday I went to-to-to ch-church for the first t-t-time. This is only my-my-my s-second t-t-time, my-my first crusade-meet-t-ting."

To my astonishment, he then announced to the entire congregation, "That young man is blessed. He has received the grace of God. Yes, you, young man. God's favor is on you."

Then he said to the congregation most persuasively, "It is so much better to receive God's wondrous grace while you are young."

How deeply grateful was my heart to know that I had received something, even though I had no idea what grace was. I thought, *Look at me, I don't have anything, no decent clothes, no money, no family status, nothing to be proud about.* And I wondered, *What could it mean to receive the grace of God–maybe a new suit of clothes?* But I did not see any clothes anywhere that someone else was not already wearing.

After the meeting, the guest preacher came to me and asked, "Are you going to stay for the overnight prayer meeting tonight?"

Because of my great respect for him, I bowed and said, "Yes," even though I would not know what to do at such a meeting. But I remained there with ten others, and learned that the best way to pray to God is loud.

By Tuesday morning, I was suffering such agony from the knowledge of sin that I went alone to a nearby mountain, where I stayed all day, then all night, weeping and shouting my confession of sin to God. There was such a load of sin in my life–so much hatred and anger, so much sadness and resentment, such a deep desire for revenge, so many twisted visions of violence, murder, death, and dying at the hands of men and from hideous diseases, so much torment. I tried to work through my great internal suffering, repenting very hard though not even knowing how to pray, just weeping and pleading, "God, please forgive my sins, forgive my sins."

By early Wednesday morning, after that lonely all-night prayer vigil, I knew I either had to confess to the lay minister, Hyung Tae Kim, how desperate I was, and ask him to pray that my soul would be saved–or die.

He welcomed me, prayed for me gladly and fervently, then said, "Young man, the Lord has already saved you. He has washed away all your sins from your whole life. You are forgiven. You don't have to be sad anymore. You are now a child of God. Why don't you give thanks to God and be joyful?"

I looked up at him, amazed. I had been a lost sinner, burning alive in a relentless desert, and he had led me to the Fountain of Living Water. When I finally comprehended that what he said was true, I sank to my knees sobbing and shouting, "Thank You! Thank You! Thank You, God! Now I know who I am: I am a child of God. Thank You, thank You, God!" As I gained momentum, rocking back and forth, back and forth, with rivers of tears streaking my cheeks and hands, praising

God and thanking Him over and over for forgiving all my sins, suddenly my tongue curled up and I began to utter foreign and unfamiliar sounds which I could not understand, as if my tongue were twisting in its own strange dance. I did not know what it was, but I kept doing it, and I kept listening to it, and I kept praying in my mind, *If this is from You, God, then it is all right with me. If this is from You, help me to do it more even if my jaw falls off. If it is not from You, stop me! Stop me!*

He did not stop me, and I prayed in those strange and amazing sounds for an hour with my mind perfectly sober but my entire body aflame. After the first hour, the strange sounds settled into a recognizable though still unfamiliar language. The prayer lasted for eight more hours during which I saw man-size angels coming down to the platform at the front of the sanctuary and walking around. I saw vast fields of grain ripen before my eyes, then angels came again and walked around. In case I might be dreaming, I stretched my eyes wide open, but still the visions remained for a full eight hours, until the evening service began at 8:30.

I had eaten nothing all day. No matter, I stayed. During the meeting, the guest preacher shocked me again by announcing to the congregation, "That young man prayed in 'other tongue.' It is written in the Bible that when the Holy Spirit comes upon you, you too will speak in new tongue–like him."

Written in the Bible? Ah, I was elated that the grace I had received from God somehow connected me with the Bible. I did not own a Bible because, in the first place, I had never thought about owning one before. In the second place, I did not know anybody who did own one. All the people I knew living there in the far countryside were too poor to own such things. But some members of that Presbyterian church owned Bibles.

I wanted so much to read for myself the part about speaking in other tongues that I waited until that meeting ended, then asked one of the church elders, "Would you lend me your Bible so I can read about other tongue in the Bible?"

He graciously consented. But when I asked him where in the Bible was the Scripture that showed about speaking in other tongues, he seemed puzzled, then said, "No, don't read the Bible that way. Read from beginning to end. You'll find it. You can borrow my Bible for one week and find it for yourself."

I thanked him, then followed his advice. Starting with Genesis, in one week I read the Bible through to the end. In the New Testament, when I found several verses confirming that we would speak in other tongues (Acts 10:46; 19:1-6, 1 Cor. 12:10; 14:5), I jumped up and down, clapped my hands, shouted, danced, and cried, so excited, so thankful to God that my experience was written about in the Bible.

The next Sunday morning, I was still so happy that I returned to the Methodist church before the service to clean all the muddy shoes lined up outside the door. After the service, I returned the Bible to its Presbyterian owner down the street, and went to a different person to borrow another Bible for the next week.

Each week for ten weeks, I borrowed a different Bible and read it front to back, and cover to cover. Every day, after first attending early morning prayer, I swept the Methodist churchyard, then began reading. I read the Bible in the daytime, in the nighttime, while walking down the street, standing up, sitting down on the floor eating, and even perched on the rim of the big ceramic jar in the toilet house. And in there the worst thing that could happen, happened. I dropped the borrowed Bible. What could I do? I fished it out, then carefully washed every page clean with running water at the town pump. By then it was waterlogged. I knew that even after it dried out, it would still be swollen out of shape. I could not return it to the owner in that condition. Not knowing what else to do, I kept that one for myself, scraped together all the money I could lay my hands on, and purchased a replacement to give to the owner. And that is how I came to possess my first very own Bible.

Five

God's Inscrutable Ways

If I must boast, I will boast of the things that show my weakness. ...so that Christ's power may rest on me. ...For when I am weak, then I am strong. 2 Corinthians 11:30; 12:9d,10d NIV

1957–1959: Yesan

It was during that Christmas season, while the carefully washed pages of my first very own Bible were drying out, when I decided to experiment with fasting-prayer for six days under the church. That was when I became trapped and had to be rescued by the pastor and the other men.

Shortly after that, my aunt began urging me to start thinking about getting married. But I thought, *How can I get married? I already have to feed all these people. I am only twenty. If I marry a younger woman, she will leave her family to join mine. I would just be adding another orphan to this already orphanage situation.*

My undaunted aunt, however, had someone special in mind for me—Kang Soon, a shy young woman five years older than I, who had already been a Christian for six years. After her parents died, Kang Soon, the only daughter in her family, had moved down from Seoul to Yesan to be raised by her mother's Buddhist family. Korean Buddhists assume a financial burden to serve the dead through religious observances with food, incense and gifts on special days, and it becomes very expensive. Kang Soon's aunt, therefore, recommended that Kang Soon become involved socially at the Methodist church, rather than at the Buddhist temple, because Christians have no such costly obligations.

Kang Soon obeyed. But she soon gave her heart to the Lord, and her entire family began persecuting her for attending the Christian church, while they remained Buddhists. Consequently, she was very lonely.

Since she was also of the age to marry, her Methodist church family, who loved her, warned her not to marry a non-Christian man. In a town the size of Yesan, where everybody knew everybody else—who was Christian and who was not—she did not have many eligible men to choose from. To help her out, her elder cousin-brother, a dentist in the remote village of Kwang-si, introduced her to a young, single dentist. But he was not a Christian, so she refused to marry him.

Kang Soon was actively involved in the Yesan Methodist Church. She not only taught Sunday school to the children, but rain, snow or shine she also never missed attending the daily 4 a.m. prayer meeting that I also attended. Even though we belonged to the same small church of only about 300 adult members, because of Korean custom we had never spoken. To forestall gossip, men and women sat on opposite sides of the sanctuary, and had no verbal communication with each other at all.

Every morning after early prayer, I first swept the churchyard, then helped at the church in whatever way I could find. The members liked me even though I was still shamed by not having parents or family status, and by my poverty and serious stutter. I did not like to appear at church-group meetings, fearful of maybe being elected again as a leader, as I had been in evening school. I could help other people, but I was afraid to stand and talk in front of them. Consequently, despite my aunt's urging, when I first noticed Kang Soon and saw how well respected she was in the church for her behavior, I decided that she was not someone I could ever approach, much less try to speak to.

Kang Soon lived in a house with a tile roof and was high up in the social strata, while I was lower than the lowest. But my aunt was persistent. Disregarding our unequal social status, she decided that Kang Soon would make me a good wife. She had already spoken to an older woman minister about it, and that woman spoke to Kang Soon. As a result, the minister and my aunt arranged for us to meet formally in my aunt's house, where we were prevailed upon to talk to each other. At that meeting, Kang Soon was so pleasant and humble, I liked her immediately, and the people around us encouraged us to become engaged. And while I still had no idea of what she thought of me, that is how our engagement was arranged.

As an engaged man I needed to work. I had already qualified to become a government official by passing the very difficult and extensive government examinations, which covered mathematics, geography, science, literature, and Chinese history and culture. But the meager salary from this position would not support a family. Therefore, when I discovered that a former teacher of mine was prospering in the poultry business, I decided that I too would go into the prosperous poultry business.

With support from the Stock Breeders Association and in partnership with my elder brother, I built mud-brick walls, and wire and wood chicken coops and pigpens, then bought 5,000 chicks, 30 piglets and 100 ducklings. I was soon working long and hard selling chicken eggs and duck eggs, live chickens and live piglets, plucked chickens and slaughtered pigs in the open-air market in town and delivering door-to-door. After two years, the business began to flourish, for which I gave all thanks to God. But the non-Christian members of my own family scorned my attitude of praise and thanksgiving, saying, "He claims he is prospering now just because he believes in Jesus. But see how hard he has to work!"

Sadly, while the poultry business prospered, the Yesan Methodist Church finances floundered. During the previous several years, Pastor Oh had made twelve separate, tearful pleas to his congregation for contributions to complete the desperately needed new sanctuary. The old one was literally falling to pieces under their feet. Long before I joined the church, when he first asked his members to finance a new structure on the church property, his attendance dropped almost overnight from close to 700 to below 250 adult members. After I joined, the church grew some, but there were still only about 300 loyal members left.

My heart grieved for him as I watched the members refuse to give. I gave all I could whenever I could, and when my third major contribution barely touched the need, I impulsively borrowed money on the poultry business to boost the church budget over the top.

Except for my Christian mother and younger brothers, who faithfully attended the church, the rest of my family continually ridiculed and mocked what they considered my foolhardy commitment to the invisible Jesus and the visibly disintegrating church, and they moved away from us into the homes of other relatives.

At home I was still "king." I was learning much from the Scriptures and could be told nothing, while at the same time growing more and more morbidly suicidal because of the unrest in my spirit. Regardless of my inner turmoil, however, I struggled to hold on to the business.

Early in 1959, I was drafted into the South Korean Army, but stayed at camp for only ten days before they rejected me because of my flat feet. The authorities had determined that a person with flat feet cannot walk long distances, and is, therefore, unfit for military combat. Mortified, I returned home to the pigs and chickens, unaware that a momentous change was about to occur in my life.

In May 1959, I heard about a six-day evangelistic crusade sponsored by my Methodist church, to be held a month later in Taechon on Seongju Mountain, about thirty-two miles south of Yesan, and I began praying that I might take part in it. But, when the time arrived, because of hectic business matters I could not go for the Monday session. Without allowing myself the luxury of disappointment, I prayed more diligently to the Lord to be able to go for Tuesday. When I also could not go for Tuesday, I prayed again for Wednesday. Unable to attend Wednesday or Thursday or Friday, at last

I was able to leave on Friday afternoon, arriving at about 11 p.m., in time to be involved for only one hour on Saturday morning, but giving thanks to God for the opportunity to participate at all. I prayed with the others for that one final hour, then returned home later in the day.

While I was up there, a refined, wealthy woman down in Yesan was praying for her tiny, two-year-old daughter who had suffered for three months from a painful condition where she had been passing more than seven fluid ounces of water every day. The child had become so dehydrated that her doctors despaired of her recovery. But God spoke to the mother while she was praying, and said, "Invite Ki Dong Kim, who is even now praying on the mountain. He will be back down this afternoon. Ask him to heal your daughter. He is My chosen servant to heal the sick in My name."

Upon my return, she told me what the Lord had said to her. I was stunned. I did not know how I could heal a sick child–or anyone, for that matter. I had never prayed for the sick, nor had I myself received such a revelation as hers. I only knew in my head that Jesus healed a blind man by touching his eyes, and that He said, "And these signs will accompany those who believe: In my name they will drive out demons...speak in new tongues...place their hands on sick people, and they will get well" (Mk. 16:17,18 NIV).

Unable to doubt the woman's vision or that the Lord had spoken to her in that strange manner, I went to her home. When I entered the room, I saw the baby drowsy and pale, laboring to breathe. As the child's distraught mother stood by weeping and wringing her hands, I could only pray to God silently, *Lord, You know I have never experienced healing the sick. But if You told this lady that You will use me to heal her sick child, You better let me know it.*

Instantly, in a riveting vision I saw myself dressed in white and standing before the presence of Almighty God. Shaken and thus emboldened, I fearfully touched the baby's sides with trembling hands, closed my eyes, and beseeched the Lord with all of my heart and with quavering in my voice, "Lord God, may Your miracles happen to this baby. Please answer my prayer and that will be enough! May Your miracles happen to this baby. Please answer my prayer. It will be enough!"

After praying the same prayer over and over, when I felt it was finally completed, I stopped speaking, opened my eyes, and looked at the baby. At the same instant, the baby opened her eyes wide and looked at me. We all could see by the bright sparkle in her eyes that God had truly touched her. I rejoiced greatly with the mother, and praised and thanked the Lord for His all-encompassing mercy and compassion, and for His healing power.

Overwhelmed and humbled, I returned home, still praising the Lord, and repeating over and over, "Thank You, Lord! Thank You, Lord! Thank You, Lord, for using me and for answering my prayer."

The next day, the astonished doctors declared the baby's healing a true miracle.

A few months later, when a typhoid epidemic was spreading throughout our village, a deaconess asked me to accompany her to the home of a family of five. We arrived there before dawn while nobody else was nearby. The Public Health Center officials had already posted a quarantine warning and cordoned off the property with their officially marked straw ropes. We ducked under the rope, entered the house, and found all five members of the family lying prostrate on the floor, covered with blankets. Two of them appeared close to death.

Once again I prayed, "Lord, if You chose me to heal the sick, may Your miracles be allowed to happen to this family." Then I placed my hands on their foreheads one by one, and prayed for them individually. Amazingly, as soon as I touched them, their fevers broke. They kicked off their blankets and bounded up onto their feet, shouting, "I'm healed! I'm healed!"

After that, many, many other miracles occurred through me. I had never before witnessed such miracles; only in the Bible had I read about such things happening. Experiencing them myself, I felt as though I had entered a different world. And, from that moment on, I prayed earnestly that God would continue to use me to bring healing to His people and glory to His name.

Six

Deliverance From Chickens

...as thy days, so shall thy strength be.
Deuteronomy 33:25b

1959–1960: Yesan

I spent all my days reading the Bible, praying, working hard at the chicken farm, and serving the Methodist church, while grieving over the financial bind still holding back completion of the new sanctuary. Even while the pastor pleaded with his members and they wept together with him, the money barely trickled in, and the stop-and-go construction dragged on for over five years. But the day finally came in 1959, when we chiseled the last of the four 100-pound triangular stone blocks needed to support the top of the bell tower. We had been so frugal with our construction funds, that our one and only roof-high, moveable scaffold-ladder was weatherworn–splintered and splitting from rain, snow, sleet, and drastic temperature changes. It had already undergone major repairs several times. Tragically, an elderly hired construction worker had fallen from the top to his death. Another man, young and very strong, had with extreme difficulty and risk hauled the first block up the rungs to the top of the tower. But as soon as his feet again touched solid earth, he threw himself facedown on the ground and vowed never to climb up there again, not for all the tea in China.

As hard as we tried, we could not even hire one day laborer willing to do what needed to be done, so I decided that I must do it myself, accepting before God all responsibility for any missteps I might take.

Before I started, I knelt down and prayed aloud, "Lord, I am Yours! You saved me, a worthless sinner, so put Your heavy burdens on me that I may do the work others are not willing to do. Give it to me as my portion. I will take charge of it, even to my death."

Wondering whether I was weak in my mind, the other workers loaded one of the remaining three stone blocks onto my bony back, and I cautiously started the climb up the old and rotting rungs. Halfway up, I looked down. The road beneath me spun crazily, so I prayed again louder than before, "Lord, help! I am weak! Give me Your strength. Charge me with this work that the others cannot do, and give me the ability to do it."

The higher I climbed, the more the blustery autumn wind shook and rattled the ladder. Finally, I unloaded the stone at the top and went back down for the next one. Praying in the spirit continually, while the others also prayed and watched in awe, I hoisted the next stone up and onto my back by myself, and carried it all the way up the creaking ladder, then came back down again.

With supernatural strength I hauled the last of the four stones up to the top. But as soon as I gained the ground for the last time and moved away, the ladder collapsed at midpoint and crashed down behind me into a heap of decayed wood and splintered boards. Only the angels of God could have sustained it that long.

After that time, every drudgery of the church became my assignment, and I worked in silence with gratitude to God for the use of His strength to do what had to be done. But I was becoming proud of the way God was using me. It was my time for a humbling.

On December 22, 1960, my brothers and married sisters gathered together with the rest of us in Yesan for a memorial ceremony for our father, who had been dead for seven years. Since our mother, my younger brothers and I were all believers in the Lord Jesus Christ, we wanted a simple church service, but my stubborn elder brother insisted on a costly, sacred, Buddhist ancestor-worship ceremony. Even though that brother was not a true believer in Buddha, his argument was that our father's disembodied spirit would otherwise be relegated to eternal wandering in space.

Like true male descendants of the yangban, we argued back and forth for hours. At three o'clock in the morning, I determined to make an end of the quarreling, and shouted at him, "God has blessed us so much that today we can all gather here together. It is owing to God's support and His blessing alone that our poultry business is prospering. Well, admit it!"

My elder brother flared up. "I thought you were so clever! Why do you say it is God Who does this work? You and I—we achieved today's success because we work diligently. Admit it! Did God bring us money? Where is it? When did we receive any money from God?"

The argument had gone on long enough. With a loud voice I spoke clearly and finally to him. I said, "My elder brother, you are profaning the God Who blesses us. I will prove to you whether or not our business was developed only through our efforts. If this be so, nothing out of the ordinary will happen tonight. However, if this success is from what God has given us, He will take back His possessions from in front of your eyes, and you will know it without question!"

After making that final declaration, I crossed in front of him to the other side of the room, and lay down on the floor by myself as if to sleep. But as soon as the others went out, I got back up on my knees and prayed to the Lord: "O Lord, I have no doubt that everything we have is what You have given us. So, if that is true, please take away all those things tonight that are from You alone. Thus there will be repenting in my household, and it will be a sure token that all our blessings come from Your hand. Amen."

I awoke in the morning to my mother's shrieks and cries and my elder brother's shouts and curses. During the night, an incredible thing had happened. Thousands of yesterday's 86-percent egg-laying hens lay dead in heaps across the chicken yard like piles of fallen leaves. The thirty or more still alive were contorting and writhing and screeching hideously. At our pig farm, at least thirty pigs had died overnight, including some of our healthiest young piglets. In just those three hours before dawn, according to my words, our hope of the poultry industry lay shattered, and my home rocked with the sounds of weeping and wailing, with curses and accusations.

Even I was stunned. Furious, I shouted at my family members again: "Look what you have done! Look at this! What did I say? Didn't I say that God's property would be taken from the home which denies His blessing on it? It was done just as I said last night."

Then I sat down on the floor and, while still weeping from the shock, prayed to God, thanking Him from my heart for such an evidence of faith and His direct response to my specific prayer. At the same time, my entire household grumbled and groaned as in the wake of a tidal wave of tears. But I could only thank God sincerely in my heart for such a display of His power and His displeasure.

One of the male relatives disposed of the dead chickens, while believers from the church consoled me in this "tragic accident." Strange as it seemed, I never felt any sense of misfortune over the horrendous results of my prayer. But for the next two-and-a-half years, heaven was closed to me. My prayers fell back upon me unanswered as if God had forsaken me for such presumption. Still, I leaned completely upon Him. In spite of His silence, I prayed all day every day, while ambling down the streets, or sitting up all night, or lying prostrate on the side of a hill. Never once in my great sorrow did I find a trace of resentment against Him in my heart, for He is the Rock. His works are perfect. All His ways are just. I find no fault in Him (Deut. 32:4, Jn. 19:4).

Seven

Kang Soon

...there is nothing covered, that shall not be revealed; and hid, that shall not be known.

Matthew 10:26

1960–1962: Yesan, Seoul, Yesan

In spite of God's silence as solid as brass, I leaned completely upon Him, praying, praying always for His mercy and His favor. He is very life to me. Whatever might happen to me, "The Lord is righteous in all his ways, and holy in all his works" (Ps. 145:17).

After the ruin of our poultry farm, I searched for other work, but no jobs were available. I wandered about with no place to claim as my own, roaming the streets, praying, always praying to recover God's blessing. My mind was in agony, tormented by the Scripture:

> *Then shall they call upon me, but I will not answer; they shall seek me early, but they shall not find me*
> (Prov. 1:28).

It seemed clear that God had forsaken me.

Attempting to rebuild my life, I took stock of my potential. I knew I had talent for drawing and painting, so with just the little amount of money left from selling what I could salvage of the poultry business, I purchased brushes, paint supplies, and other equipment, and began drawing and painting pictures to sell, including a series of eighteen three-dimensional oil paintings, depicting dramatic scenes from the Bible. My friends convinced me to display them first in the recently completed First Methodist Church building, then twice at our local tea house. At all three exhibitions people admired them greatly, and bought almost all of them. The rest I gave away.

Then I discovered I had talent in portraiture–able to draw and paint detailed portraits almost like photographs, completing four in a single day. One day, I painted beautiful portraits for a couple who hired me, but as soon as they put money in my hand, I felt empty, as though I had just sold my virginity in the marketplace. After that day, though I still took delight in painting, I never again painted for money. I longed for everything I did to be only for the pleasure of the Lord.

Some members of the American Consulate, who came to view my exhibits, acknowledged my talent in painting, and one of them offered to finance my study in the United States at Pratt Institute in New York City. But as much as I dreamed and prayed to study abroad, our civilian government under Syngman Rhee permitted no adult Korean male to travel abroad until after completing three years of military service in the South Korean Army.

Hastily, I again enlisted, but again the Army brass rejected me because of my flat feet. I re-enlisted again and again, so determined was I to serve my country in order to go abroad to study art. But each time I was rejected for the same two flat feet. Finally, when I was about to enlist for the sixty-eighth time, I was drafted by the peace-time Army, only to be rejected again on the final day of selection.

Well, maybe I was not meant to be a decorated soldier, maybe not a famous artist, maybe not a successful poultry farmer, but there was something else I knew I could try. In spite of my eternally disheartening stutter, I knew I could teach. With just enough money saved to move up to Seoul, in March 1960, I enrolled at Seoul Teachers College, and began my pursuit of a certificate to teach school.

Then, in May 1961, at the end of my very first year in college, Generals Park, Chung Hee and Toyon Chang overthrew the civilian government in a military coup, and the new military government decided that anyone who had not served in the Army was also not qualified to be a teacher. So I had to give up that idea, too.

But all was not lost. Four years earlier in 1957, I had passed the government examinations, and still qualified to become a government official. However, when I inquired, I found that the salary offered for that position still would not be enough to support the people I had to support. So, before I could be assigned to a position in the government in Seoul, I quickly retreated to Yesan. But I need not have hurried. The governing military then issued the order that anyone who had not served in the Army did not qualify for any position in the new government.

Once again I re-enlisted and once again was rejected. By late 1961, besides being drafted twice, I had tried to enlist in the South Korean Army sixty-eight times. Apparently, the only way for me to survive in Korea was to work day labor. However, at that time there were not enough day-labor wages to go around. By then completely discouraged, I gave up hope, and felt once again for the comforting presence of the quinine pills in my pocket.

Meanwhile, without my knowledge, my persistent aunt kept going to Kang Soon and pleading with her: "You have to help him out. He needs your help." Each time she put Kang Soon on the spot like that, Kang Soon asked her, "How can I help him? Everything he tries, he fails. My family tells me he is hopeless, and that I should forget about him. I am already old enough to marry. If I wait on him…"

But my aunt was not dissuaded even from using unfair tactics on Kang Soon, and she would say, "I appeal to your motherly heart. You have to take care of him." Put in such a difficult position, Kang Soon finally agreed to work to support me. To do so, she moved south to Kwang-si to work as a dental technician near her cousin-brother, the dentist. Knowing that she was skilled and good at making money, he helped her open her own business in his office, where she would find good, paying customers.

According to Korean tradition, it was shameful for an unmarried man to visit an unmarried woman, but I nevertheless visited her there often; and the more my already great respect for her grew, the more I could not imagine what she could possibly see in me.

On a cold winter day late in February 1962, I followed her from her workplace on the main street of Kwang-si up a big hill to the house where she rented a room from a family named Kim. They had not known Kang Soon was engaged until she introduced me to them. But then, since we shared the same family name and the same ancestors, they treated me like their own son-in-law, talking to me and preparing a big feast. They did not know my motive for coming was to see Kang Soon one last time before I committed suicide. I hoped that then I would be with Jesus and out of my misery.

While I was there, the temperature outside dropped below freezing, and the Kims invited me to stay overnight.

Since my one-and-only jacket was light summer-weight, and my only shoes thin cotton sneakers, I gladly accepted their invitation. After dinner, I hung my jacket in Kang Soon's room, joined the other family members for the evening conversation, then slept for the night in another room with the other males.

The next morning, when I told Kang Soon goodbye, I hoped she could not read in my face the decision I had already made. I put on my jacket, then walked down the narrow path to the main street to catch the bus back to Yesan. I could almost feel her watching me, but I never looked back. I kept my eyes focused straight ahead, determined to end my life that very morning; I did not want to falter again, to be dissuaded by the sight of her eyes watching me going away from her. I had nothing to offer her. She would be better off with somebody else.

I had determined to go to a particular spot on the left bank of Won Creek, a small stream near Yesan, where there was sand and grass and trees, a good place to lie down to take the pills. It would only take a few, and I had accumulated seven times more than enough.

When I arrived at that place, I sat down near the water and reached for the package in my pocket. This was it. I untied the package and poured the contents into my hand, then stared. I could not believe my eyes.

Eight

My Ways, Not Your Ways

A man's heart deviseth his way: but the Lord directeth his steps. Proverbs 16:9

February–March 1962: Yesan

What my eyes told me could not be true! Instead of pills, my hand was full of money.

Immediately, I knew, "This comes from my wife!" and I was crowned with shame. It is Korean tradition that the man who is engaged to a woman should take care of that woman, but I had no way to do that. Actually, at that moment I did not have enough money of my own to replace the pills she had taken—no, not taken! She had bought them out of my pocket, the ultimate humiliation. I did not know what to do. I did know that I could not use her money for pills!

Filled with insecurities and deep despair, I knew there was a way. I stopped having my hair cut, and saved enough money that way to replace the thirty pills

Kang Soon had taken out of my pocket. Druggists, however, are not utter fools: Quinine pills are so poisonous, no Korean druggist would sell more than a few to any one person at one time without a doctor's prescription. I had to visit back and forth between three different drug stores to finally replace them slowly by twos and threes.

Meanwhile, Kang Soon, who also was no fool, convinced her brother to set our wedding date up to March 31, the last day of the very next month. When I was told, I interpreted that as part of her plan to manipulate the rest of my life, and it infuriated me. I did not know any other way to punish her except to kill myself before the March date arrived.

I still read my Bible every day, loving God with all my heart, but truly seeking Him with only half my mind. The other half was absorbed with plotting total liberation from my circumstances. All the negative, discouraging aspects of my personal life and all our stifling Korean traditions crowded in upon me: Strong desire to escape was my only motivation. All other roads were dead ends; I could see no other way out. I even cried out to God for His help. "Take my life!" He answered not a word, so I knew I would have to do it myself.

A few days later, I went alone up to a wooded area in the center of Seoul City, but there were people everywhere. So I climbed to the very top of South Mountain, then walked down slowly, seeking the most secluded place I could find with a thick layer of fallen leaves. I would slide underneath them, cover myself up, take my pills, and quietly die. There my body would disintegrate and simply disappear into the ground. Nobody would ever find it. No one would even miss me—except maybe the hard-working, always praying, inscrutable Kang Soon, but she would survive.

When I found a suitable place in the remotest area of the mountain, another distraught man suddenly showed up alongside of me. Obviously at the end of his rope, he had come groaning and moaning to that same place for the same reason I had come, to destroy himself. In one hand he held a letter to his wife explaining the reasons for his death—what a failure he was, and how she could get along better without him. In his other hand, a dozen easily recognizable quinine pills.

I heard his heart breaking in the agony of his soul. "No, no!" I shouted, surprising even myself. "Don't do it!" I said. "If you have enough sense to figure out how to collect all those pills, use that same sense to live!"

As I heard my own words, it was as though I admonished myself. Then, when the man got up and disappeared through the woods, I realized that my own resolve to die that very day had broken down along with his.

Still, I wandered around for days, not knowing what to do or which way to turn, while my God said nothing to me.

Soon after that, again motivated by a desire to escape, I climbed to the top of a cliff overhanging the Han River. From there I could leap into the rocky riverbed below and drown in the deep and turbulent waters. Weeping in sorrow, I sat down on the top-most ledge. A young woman on the same ledge a few yards away sat hunched over and cried so pitifully, I knew that she too planned to throw herself over the edge to her death. I scrambled over to her, crying loudly, "No, no! Don't do it! If you have the courage to jump, use that courage to live!" Then, like the man earlier, she too stood to her feet and hurried back down the mountain.

On a third occasion, which I had decided was my final opportunity, I met another very distraught man ready to kill himself, and this time I stopped him by saying, "Believe in Jesus! If you believe in Jesus, you will not want to die!"

Instantly, that man simply disappeared. Shocked and shamed, I began to mourn and to weep, suddenly realizing that those three despondent people were in fact God's answer to my cry for help—not hopeless cases sent for me to minister to them, but messengers of God ministering to me through my own words: "Use your sense to live! Have courage! Believe in Jesus!" No doubt they were God's angels, "...ministering spirits sent to serve those who will inherit salvation" (Heb. 1:14 NIV). But was I one who would inherit salvation?

Sadly, the irony of my situation remained; I had lost all joy and longed for death, when suddenly other passages of Scripture began to hound me, locking my soul in torment:

> *...every sin and blasphemy will be forgiven men, but the blasphemy against the Spirit will not be forgiven. Anyone who speaks a word against the Son of Man will be forgiven, but anyone who speaks against the Holy Spirit will not be forgiven, either in this age or in the age to come. ...*[For] *It is impossible for those who have once been enlightened, who have tasted the heavenly gift, who have shared in the Holy Spirit, who have tasted the goodness of the word of God and the powers of the coming age, if they fall away, to be brought back to repentance, because to their loss they are crucifying the Son of God all over again and subjecting him to public disgrace* (Mt. 12:31,32, Heb. 6:4-6 NIV).

Surely, in some way I had blasphemed the Holy Spirit and subjected the beloved Son of God to public disgrace. There was no hope for me in either living or dying.

Nine

Wife

Moreover as for me, God forbid that I should sin against the Lord in ceasing to pray for you.
1 Samuel 12:23a

March 31–April 1, 1962: Yesan, Sung-hwan National Forest

When General Park began his rule in 1962, South Korea began rousing herself from her deep national depression. But not me. Having failed to rouse myself from my deep personal depression, and having failed three times to end my life because of it, when I realized that Kang Soon had set our wedding date up, not to manipulate me, but to preempt my suicide, I simply gave in. I surrendered to her plans. My wife-to-be was determined to support me by herself. But why? I still could not understand her. According to Korean custom, any woman who supports her husband relinquishes all rights to any kind of support for herself from within her own extended family. As long as she remains in her family, she is not allowed to support a husband. So for me the questions remained: Why was Kang Soon willing to submit to that? Why marry me? What did she see in me?

Our wedding day finally arrived, the day before my life would be turned upside down forever in ways I could never have imagined.

Kang Soon had been attending the Kwang-si Baptist Church because there was no Methodist church in that area. We were married, however, at the First Methodist Church in Yesan, but not in the costly traditional way of Korean weddings with a great spread of food prepared for the guests to take back home with them. Ours was a simple Christian ceremony with only our relatives and dear church family as witnesses. Some brought gifts, including enough money for me to buy a real suit for the occasion—my one-and-only suit for years to come—a heavy, black winter-wool, three-piece suit.

Kang Soon was no doubt more beautiful than ever in her formal, Western-style, long, white bridal gown, but I was too dull to notice. I felt stupid and hopeless even being there, the bridegroom who could not support a wife or family, who had no home, no job, no anything. My side of the family was so poor that there had been no money to buy a proper wedding ring. I was about to enter the wedding hall without a ring until one of my female relatives stopped me, removed her own ring from her finger, and lent it to me until after the ceremony, when I returned it to her.

As was Korean custom, after the ceremony, my bride donned a traditional Korean wedding dress to bow before our parents. After the wedding supper, we went to her parents' house where–also Korean custom–we all slept together in one room. The next morning, since there was no money for a honeymoon-hotel, we ended up at the train station heading in opposite directions. The villagers, who always knew everything about everybody, watched us with wry amusement, remarking how strange it was that, the day after the wedding, Kang Soon purchased only one ticket to Kwangsi. They wondered aloud why she was going back alone to the room she had prepared for us to live in as husband and wife.

My excuse was that I preferred to please God rather than follow my wife to where she worked to support me (too embarrassing). Therefore, I had decided to go eight miles in another direction to the Sung-hwan National Forest near my oldest sister's home to pray there without the distraction of my bride.

While Kang Soon and I stood together waiting for her train, she finally said to me, "I have something to say to you. May I speak?"

With no idea of what was on her mind, I said, "Go ahead."

She looked straight into my eyes for a moment, then respectfully lowered her eyes and began speaking. "For a long time before I came to a certain age, I prayed a lot to God, 'Please God, when it is right time, tell me whom to marry.' Then one day as I was crossing the river on the flat-stone bridge, something like big picture appeared in front of my eyes, and I saw Christian young man standing before me, but I had never seen that person. Even earlier than that, I had seen small vision of same person, but this time I could not deny because it was very big picture, one that covered very wide field.

"I prayed a lot to have good marriage with Christian young man. Then, I began hearing much about such a man with very strong faith, a hard worker for the church, but I did not know who he was.

"Then you came to that church, very poor and not much to show, and when I saw your face, that you were the one I saw two times in the visions, I was shocked. Christians in the church said to me, 'That young man is the one who received the grace of God in the crusade-meeting.' I would never consider two visions as determining factor of whom to marry, just reference. But after I decided to marry you, I remembered them.

"Then you visited me in Kwang-si where I lived in the Kims' house. As soon as you were sleeping in other room, I started praying, and during my prayer your jacket hanging on my wall drew my attention. I felt fear in the spirit that there was some awful thing with your jacket. So I went to the jacket and put my hand into the pocket, and felt something wrapped in paper, like beans wrapped up. I opened it up and found your pills inside, and…"

I had heard enough, so naturally I interrupted. "It is Korean tradition for woman not to put hand in man's pocket because man is above woman and leader of the family!"

Surprisingly, Kang Soon quietly continued as though I had not spoken. "I saw that you had intention to commit suicide, and I felt terrified finding that out. I was there working hard to support you, not for myself but for you. Still…"

Again I interrupted. "It is Korean tradition…!"

"I know," she said, looking up at me. "Still, I felt that I had to do it." She looked back down. "When I found those terrible things in my hand, they made me tremble. So I kept those pills to myself, and put the money into the pocket instead."

I was so surprised, I could not think how to rebuke her, so I stood as tall as I could and glowered down at the top of her head. She said nothing more, but bowed respectfully, then turned and walked away. Stunned and angry, I glared daggers at her back as she walked toward the train that would take her to her workplace. Then I too turned and, to the sound of shrieking steam whistles signaling the departure that would separate me from my wife-of-one-day, I too walked away—to the train that would take me to the mountain.

Alone for forty days in the dense mountain forest, nourished only by the one meal a day my sister brought up to me, I prayed with tears and deep sighing. I prayed about the dismal failure of my life. I prayed for God to bless Kang Soon and me with a child—a son—while trembling in fear that another miserable "me" might be born with a destiny like mine, in every aspect a loser. Fearing that I would be an ineffectual father unable to raise him properly, I prayed earnestly that unlike me my son would be born with God's blessing. I prayed that God would take him and use him only for His purposes. I surrendered total responsibility to Almighty God to train my son as one of His workers.

But how dare I pray such a thing? In Korea at that time, to be a worker for God meant starvation and agony of soul. Still, how could I not? Did I not trust Him? Oh yes, I trusted Him to do only wondrous things, as His Word promises (Ps. 72:18). And so, even before my son was conceived, by a conscious act of my will out on that wild and lonely mountain, I gave him to God.

Ten

Donkey

He raises the poor from the dust and lifts the needy from the ash heap; he seats them with...the princes of their people.

Psalm 113:7,8 NIV

April–June 1962: Kwang-si, Salmak Mountain, Chorong Mountain

For five years Kang Soon and I had been officially engaged to be married. Now legally married, we had spent our wedding night in a room full of relatives, after which she went back to work and I went into the mountains for forty days to pray.

After that lengthy separation, on a Saturday in mid-May, I went back down to Kang Soon in Kwang-si. With no job and no opportunity to earn money, my only choice was to rely upon her for support. I responded to my joblessness with feigned indifference. My too strong pride did not permit me to act otherwise. I felt embarrassed, humiliated, like a ram going to be dipped for ticks, so I said to my wife, "Well, you want to give me money? If you can put money in my pocket, you can give me now the tithe! I am in ministry to preach the Gospel and heal the sick, so pay the tithe to me!"

Anger lightly brushed her face, but she kept her voice low and humble. "No," she said, "the tithe goes to God's work. It belongs to Him."

About that time, the minister of the Kwang-si Baptist Church came to our house, and put special effort into inviting me to their Sunday outdoor service. But I felt morbidly sad from still living off my wife's earnings, like I should hide from the world in shame. And I complained to my wife, "How can I possibly go to the service where everyone there will be enjoying the day? How can I go out there with those happy people and play games and pretend to be in fellowship with them?"

She sighed and said, "*Yuhbo* (Honey), you are arrogant and proud and filled with self-pity. No one can tell you anything; no one can help you. Even when the pastor urges you to turn your heart to God, he knows that no one but you can change your attitude. You forget that the Bible says, '...the letter kills, but the Spirit gives life' (2 Cor. 3:6c NIV). You are killing your soul with the letter of the law, while seeking to kill your body with pills. You have turned your back on the God Who is love and on the ones who want to help you."

"But even the pastor does not know as much of the Bible as I know!" I scoffed. "I know more about the Bible than anyone else!"

"That is true, and that is very sad. I expected to find Jesus in you, my husband; that was my only reason for marrying you. But I have not yet found Him there."

I was shocked, and I said, "Well, there is nothing you can do about that now!"

"I am weak woman," she replied, "but there is one thing I can do. If nothing changes, I am leaving you. You make the decision. That is the situation, and this is my first and final notice."

I was stunned. Standing before her in my heavy wool suit with the thirty pills once again restored to my pocket, I glared at her, speechless. It is not a Korean custom for a wife to threaten her husband. It is loss-of-face for a Korean husband for his wife to give him final notice.

Then Kang Soon continued in a gentler tone. "Yuhbo, the minister understands you. He is good man. Just go with them as he asks. Restrain yourself humbly and do not talk about how much of the Bible you know. Come," she said, handing me the box of food she had prepared for the church dinner. "You should go. Don't ever feel shame." Then she gently shoved me in the direction of the departing Baptist Christians.

Stung by the ultimatum from my wife, and feeling like a bull about to be butchered, I reluctantly took the box from her hand. With all kinds of contradictions and confusing thoughts passing through my mind, I trailed behind the Baptists up the road toward Salmak Mountain. Within half an hour, something happened that turned my life around completely.

The climb became steeper and I started sweating inside my wool suit. Then suddenly, for me time stood still. Low in the sky right in front of my eyes an unaccountable phenomenon materialized seemingly out of nowhere, like nothing I had ever seen or imagined–a myriad of glowing, flashing, dazzling lights, making up one concentrated mass of ethereal brilliance no wider than four feet or taller than eighteen inches. I stood transfixed, awestruck for at least a quarter of an hour, subconsciously realizing that no one was seeing it except me. As I stood there and stared, all my fears and frustrations accumulated through the years, all my present sufferings, all desire to die were flushed away as though I were standing under a purifying waterfall.

At the same time, something extraordinary, something supernatural occurred inside my head: I heard two Scripture verses spoken to me as audibly as if an unseen preacher had read the words aloud:

> *...If you hold to my teaching, you are really my disciples. ...*[And] *If you remain in me and my words remain in you, ask whatever you wish, and it will be given you* (Jn. 8:31b; 15:7 NIV).

Stunned, I became consciously aware of another momentous truth: Even though I had read the entire Bible more than seventy-five times, never before had any of the hundreds of thousands of words come to life and taken hold of my soul like those few words did at that moment on that mountain road. I saw clearly that those two verses, separated in the Bible by almost seven full chapters, fitted together perfectly, and they spoke directly into my heart, my mind and my spirit with a thrust that moved me deeply.

God Himself was affirming and reaffirming to me that from that moment on, if I go into Him Who is the Word–go into His words, go into His words, go into His words–I will in fact be His disciple. If His words go into me–go into me, go into me–I will walk in His authority and power. I could hardly breathe from the sheer joy of that continuing revelation: Two verses–one complete experience: Going into God's words, and God's words going into me.

When I fully grasped the significance, I became sorely distressed, realizing how far short I had come from entering into and dwelling in His words. I loved all the words in the Bible, respected all of them as being from God, but I had not obeyed Him by allowing them to live in me, to control every aspect of my life. At the same time, I stood there on the mountain road, electrified by overflowing joy, as if the sky had opened and heaven's grace been poured down upon me like a flood. Now, I wanted to live! And I knew that, when this truth became fully mine indeed, no longer would I seek to become a fisher of men: I would *be* a fisher of men for God!

With that realization, I raced up the trail to the Baptist group already congregated. First, I sang them a song in my scratchy voice, then I poured out upon them the entire testimony of the phenomenon that had just occurred, and of what it meant to me: That we must no longer be preoccupied with past problems, but be totally, totally, totally immersed in and involved only with God's words. They listened, they received the message, and we rejoiced together.

On my way back down the mountain, with a sudden hilarity of joy, I realized that, had I succeeded with the poultry business, I would still be staring at chickens and waiting for eggs. If I had studied art in America, I would still be painting pictures for other people's money. If I had been accepted by the Army, I could have been killed. If I had succeeded in taking the pills...

I praised and thanked God for the many times and different ways He had stopped me and preserved my life. I praised Him all the way down to Kwang-si and my beautiful, beloved wife, Kang Soon.

Earlier that same day when I had left her, I was degraded in my own eyes and without hope. When I came down from the mountain totally overjoyed, totally a new creation altogether, Kang Soon was so shocked, so happy at the change in me, that she spent the entire night (our second night together since we were married) in the corner on her knees in prayer.

From that time on, I saw the Bible with panoramic vision–Father, Son and Holy Spirit–One God. All the histories, biographies, poems, and prophecies in the Bible came together displaying to me the many facets of its one complete revelation of our Lord Jesus Christ, Immanuel, God's unique Son, the Savior of the world.

From that time on, God's miracles multiplied:

The lay pastor in charge of Kwang-si Baptist Church invited me to go with him to visit a very sick man who was dying from tuberculosis. As soon as we entered the house, the victim, who lay prostrate on the sick bed, sat up, pointed at me, and cried out, "What happened? Somebody was lying next to me. When you came in through the door, he jumped up and ran out!" The astonished man then leapt to his feet and shouted with amazement, "My sickness is gone! My sickness is gone!" Both of his lungs had been instantly healed, a miracle later confirmed by his doctors.

The news spread. People came from all over the provinces to be healed, and the power of God moved through me like electric currents flowing through my body.

A fifteen-year-old boy, in danger of death from an attack of acute appendicitis, was instantly healed. And while his mother stood next to him, she was healed of a painful condition affecting her bones and her head.

A disfiguring lump on a young girl's face disappeared under my hand, leaving no scar.

A suicidal middle-aged man came, the whole inside of his mouth reeking from ulcerated and infected black and white sores. He was cleansed and healed and restored to his zest for life.

Attendance at the Kwang-si Baptist Church grew mightily, as those who were healed came back and brought others with them. Old people, young people and children flocked to the services in the church. Even though no one there had ever before heard of the Holy Spirit, He worked so powerfully among them that even the young children saw visions, spoke in tongues, and laid hands on each other to pray. And, even though I was only a layman, with the Baptist pastor's permission I preached sermons and prayed for the sick, and God's miracles continued to flow wherever I went.

One month after my extraordinary, life-changing experience with God's light on Salmak Mountain, being eager to attend any and all Christian meetings, I went to a Monday through Saturday evangelistic crusade led by a lady evangelist on Chorong Mountain about seven miles from Kwang-si. With no other means of transportation, several young men from the church went with me on foot. When the lady evangelist asked me to be available to pray for the sick at the early Saturday morning meeting, I stayed up all Friday night praying, praying, praying for God to give me the power to heal the sick. Three times during that night, God gave me the same vision: I saw myself standing in deep and turbulent water, casting a net. Each time I drew in the net, it came back to me full of shimmering silver fish.

The next morning at breakfast, I described the visions to the evangelist, who interpreted them for me: "You are a fisher of men," she said. "Many people will come to the Lord through you, but you will face many difficulties. In your vision, standing in deep water means much big trouble, so you can expect many in the world to come out strongly against you."

During the walk back down to Kwang-si, I was contemplating her interpretation, when I heard a man's voice call me, "Donkey! Donkey!" It was obviously not the voice of any one of my companions, so I wondered out loud, "Who is that calling me Donkey?"

I then saw in my mind the same donkey that carried Jesus into Jerusalem, how the animal had served the

Lord in perfect humility and silence, doing only what he was being led to do (Jn. 12:14,15). I knelt in the road to wait for what else God might say to me, and recalled something recorded in the Gospels that Jesus said, that even He Himself did and said nothing but what He saw and heard His Father do and say (Jn. 5:19,30). I called my companions and described what I had heard and seen, then invited them also to consider themselves as lowly, dumb donkeys accepting the bridle and bit in the service of the Lord.

As I pondered the implications further, the Lord reminded me that I was to carry only His burdens, and carry them in silence. According to my three visions in the night, I would attract much criticism from other Christians by my leading crusades, especially while still only a layman, so I was to set a watch over my mouth and never criticize anyone for any reason.

But how could I always remember that? Realizing that I would need constant reminders, I picked up a small stone by the stream and slipped it under my tongue. That impediment would surely serve as a reminder to see and hear, but to hold my peace and keep silent except when praising God and praying for the sick, never admonishing anyone in the wisdom of men's words, but only in demonstration of the Holy Spirit and in power (1 Cor. 2:4).

Then I felt God's leading: *Tell no one, but soon you are to return to Chorong Mountain alone.*

"When, Lord?"

You will know when I tell you.

"For how long, Lord?"

For ten days to fast totally and pray before Me.

Ten days of total fasting? Suddenly, I was afraid. All my life I had suffered from the effects of malnutrition. I had almost died after only six days of total fasting while trapped under the church, ten weeks after I had been born again. Since then, I had been completely delivered from all desire to commit suicide. The forty-day fast after my wedding was not a total fast, since my sister brought me food every day. But now, I feared that this trip up the mountain for ten days of total fasting from both food and water might result in my literal, physical demise at God's hand.

But God had spoken.

Eleven

Teach Me Love

For the Lord will vindicate his people and have compassion on his servants.

Psalm 135:14 NIV

May 1962: Chorong Mountain, Kwang-si, Sung-ju Mountain, Kwang-si

Two days after I returned home, a deacon surprised me by saying, "Brother Kim, if you are planning to go back up Chorong Mountain to fast and pray, I know where you can go for solitude. A big rock up there crowns a peak high over the water, and provides good shelter from the rain, the cold winds and the late snow."

I then explained to the deacon what kind of fasting-prayer God required of me–no food, no water. We both well knew the Korean superstition, "If a man goes longer than six days without food, or a woman longer than seven, that person could die." But, ten days without water? How was this possible? Searching for Scripture to confirm that I truly heard from God, I found that Jesus, Elijah and Moses had all fasted for forty days (Mt. 4:2; 1 Kings 19:8; Ex. 24:18). But did they go without water? Presumably so; Moses, explicitly so according to Exodus 34:28.

There was no denying that God had spoken to me, so the deacon agreed to pray for my safe return, as did my deeply devout wife, Kang Soon.

That same deacon accompanied me the seven miles from Kwang-si to the foot of Chorong Mountain, then led me another mile and a half up to the shelter at the top, where he left me alone.

My continual petition night and day during that time was the same: "Lord, use my life as a channel through which all lost souls might come to Your great salvation, and through whom many might be healed. God, give me Your power to love others as You love them. Give me Your power to heal."

On the third night, when I had become very weak, two small boys appeared in a vision before me. One, who carried a beautiful white kettle, said to me, "Open your mouth."

When I obeyed, he poured a little something like milk into my mouth, then both boys disappeared. For the rest of my time on the mountain, whenever I meditated on God's Word, I caught myself chewing on something (I have never found out what it was). Whenever I woke up from sleeping, I woke up chewing. After the boys disappeared, I felt neither hunger nor thirst for the last seven days of my total fast.

Meanwhile, as I prayed and shouted and shouted and prayed for God to make me a worthy example of His love, I recalled the terrifying nightmares that had tormented me while I was trapped beneath the church. I then began to understand that those dreams of my death meant that I still had to die before I could love others as Jesus loves them. But now I did not want to die! I wanted to live! I did not see how my death could solve anything, especially how it would make such love possible. And my response from God gave only partial understanding: *Die to self.*

What did it mean to die to self? I believed in my heart that healing was my job, my duty to God; and while I was there on the mountain, as I begged for the power to fulfill my duty, the Lord showed me two things: first, that healing and love cannot be separated; and second, that prayer is not an incantation, but the door to God's honorable promises and His mighty power to heal. Whatever prayer I sincerely offer to God, He receives, and I am not to blaspheme His holy name by any such insult as doubt.

I then understood that prayer is primarily my surrendering all responsibility and rights to whatever I ask for into His hands, and never, ever taking them back. I was to ask when I had nothing, so that God could create something for me.

Still, I knew my understanding was incomplete. The question on my heart remained, How can I love all men as Jesus loved? I was determined to gain full understanding.

I picked up a flat stone and positioned it precariously on a small jagged outcrop of the rock wall. With both hands I then grabbed hold of a tree branch above my head and stepped out, balancing on the small stone. I leaned my body facedown against the rocky cliffside, putting myself in a completely dead-end situation. I was that desperate to receive an answer, fully aware that unless an angel of God protected me, either the branch would break or the stone would slip, and I would plunge to my death on the rocks below. Stretched out in that helpless position, I prayed for the power to love and to serve the sick. I said aloud, "If my Lord does not answer me, I will not move from this place nor eat unto my death."

Even as the branch overhead snapped and crackled, I said to myself, *Without this determination to overcome this dead-end situation and win, I cannot do my ministry successfully.*

After one day passed with no response from God, I became anxious, thinking, *If I give up now, I won't dare to pray like this again!* Fighting the temptation to step back over on solid ground, I clung to the branch, beseeching God out loud, "What is love? Teach me to understand love! Give me the power and the ability to love and to serve the sick!"

For hours I prayed, weeping, wailing, wrestling against the nagging side of my mind that insisted over and over, *You fool! Stop now! He will not speak to you! You will fall! You will die from lack of water! You will starve to death waiting to hear from Him!* But even worse than the fear of dying was my fear that, unlike Daniel, who waited three weeks for his answer while the battle raged in the heavenlies (Dan. 10:2-13), I would give up before receiving my answer.

Still, the battle raged in my mind until I decided positively that nothing but death could change my resolve, and I shouted at myself, "Stop this fear! I will not change this prayer, and I will not leave!"

As soon as I determined decisively not to change my petition, I experienced such complete peace about dying that way, that I said out loud to myself, "All right! I will die here!"

Then at last, strong and clear understanding came to my mind: *When the Lord Jesus Christ came in His flesh, He bore no burden of His own affairs, but took others' burdens as His own, thereby willingly taking full responsibility for the results of all sins unto Himself.*

Joy filled my heart with comprehension of this astonishing truth: My responsibility to God and man was clearly twofold: first, I must surrender and relinquish all responsibility for the results of whatever I pray for into God's hands, then never take it back. I am only to apply myself to prayer, which is all I can do. Prayer is my business; answering prayer is God's business. No matter how anxious I am for the answer, there is nothing I can do to bring it about. It is God Who answers, not I. So, I will not be anxious about the results of my prayers.

Second, I must follow the example Jesus gave us of assuming responsibility unto Himself for the sins of others. This twofold responsibility to God and man was the way to love and service.

To strengthen that understanding further, I shouted to myself several times over, "Love means taking responsibility to yourself! Love means my taking responsibility for the sins of others unto myself!" Now that I knew that I knew how to love, I stepped off the rock.

As soon as I regained my footing on solid ground and let go of the branch, the loose rock flew out into the air and the brittle branch crumbled. I fell on my knees and shouted my thanks to God with all my heart and all my strength, for saving my life and broadening and strengthening my understanding of His ways.

At the end of the tenth and final day of my fast, when my friends came up the mountain to take me back home, they discovered my unconscious body, lying motionless on the stones in front of the shelter. From the appearance of my badly swollen legs and pale and ashen skin, they feared that I was dying, and quickly carried me back down to Kwang-si, where my waiting wife tended to me.

After two full weeks of painful but only partial recovery, I decided to attend a meeting to be held soon at a church on Sung-ju Mountain about twenty miles away, even if I had to walk the entire distance. And walk we did, my companions and I, while the grace of God sustained my still weak and pain-filled body all the way to the church. While there, I heard such a great testimony of God's unfailing love, I fell in agony of soul, knowing I still sorely lacked God's love.

Desperate for a resolution to that problem, I wanted more than understanding, I wanted the ability to love as Jesus loved, and the power to serve the sick. I climbed up and out onto a promontory about 150 feet up from the crusade assembly grounds, determined to wait upon God. This time, I did not look for His answer to come to my mind: I waited to hear His voice in my ear.

Hours passed. Then I heard His voice: *Go!*

It startled me. Was I hallucinating? Again and again, I prayed aloud, "God, teach me to love! Give me the power to serve the sick!"

A few minutes later, I heard the Voice again, more clearly than the first time: *Go!*

Convinced at last that it was truly His voice, I cried out, "My Lord and my God! If it is Your voice, let me hear it again!" And He said:

> *Go!* ... [And] *As you go, preach this message: 'The kingdom of heaven is near.' Heal the sick, raise the dead, cleanse those who have leprosy, drive out demons. Freely you have received, freely give* (Mt. 10:6-8 NIV).

"Yes, Lord!" I shouted. "I want to heal the sick, raise the dead, cleanse those who have leprosy, and drive out demons." And I clambered back down the rocky slope. Then my friends and I retraced our steps the entire twenty miles on foot back home to Kwang-si, where God soon gave me an opportunity to exercise what I had learned about His love and His power.

Earlier, the son of the Baptist minister had moved to another city, but he had recently come home dying with a hideous disease decaying his flesh. His father begged me, "Please, come to our home and pray for my son."

Of course I agreed, and some of our church members went with me to his home. But as soon as we opened the door, the stench from their son's body gagged us. The boy's arms and legs were filthy and swollen with poison. Since the family was poor, they had not taken him to the Christian hospital, but had treated him with traditional Korean poultices of cow dung and grasses. His body was so filthy, I was aghast, wondering, *What shall I do in this revolting situation?*

I knew I had to pray for him, so I laid my hands on his relatively clean head. Knowing full well that Jesus alone could take our infirmities and diseases into His body (Mt. 8:17), I prayed out loud dutifully if not sincerely from my heart, "L-L-Lord, if You want me to be like J-J-Jesus, and it is necessary for me to t-t-take up his illness, please remove that illness to me, and heal him. In Jesus' place, I c-c-can take up his illness."

But then a Voice spoke to one side of my mind. *Son, do you truly choose to love him? He is one of the foulest sinners you will ever see. Look! You avoid touching his dirty body, and that is why you hold his head. Yes, Jesus took your infirmities: Will you still take this disease to yourself?*

I knew the One Who was speaking to me, so with a shudder I removed my hands from the boy's head and took his swollen, encrusted and oozing hands into mine and prayed again, "L-L-Lord, if he is to d-die because of this disease, please remove th-th-this disease to me. I will t-t-take up the disease for him."

To my chagrin, the Lord then instructed me in my mind to start sucking the poison out of his arm: *If you will suck all the evil out from his arm and hand using your own mouth, new blood will appear on the surface of his skin, and that blood will heal his arm.*

What choice did I have? God had spoken. And, even as the boy screamed with pain and his parents cried and sobbed in despair, wringing their hands, and pacing back and forth, I sucked the poison out of his hand and arm until fresh blood appeared.

All during that time, a different voice on the other side of my mind kept telling me, *You better keep your eyes closed and hurry up and finish this, and wash your hands and wash out your mouth, and get out of this place.*

The two sides of my mind wrestled with each other. One side wanted desperately to flee the situation. But the other side kept praying, *Lord, l-l-l-let me take up this boy's disease. Let him l-l-live.* And I kicked the temptation to flee and kept sucking the pus out of his arms.

The boy's feet were even nastier, more revolting than his arms, but I felt compelled to suck even his feet, spitting whatever came into my mouth into the bowls his mother brought to me. After awhile, new blood appeared there as well.

All this time, the minister and his wife were weeping and wailing, and the boy had become hysterical with pain. But I kept on going, sobbing and pleading loudly with God, "Please, h-h-heal this person. If-if-if it is necessary, l-l-let me take up his d-d-disease." By that time, scabs were stuck between my teeth, but I dared not stop to spit them out for fear that my zeal for his healing would dissipate.

When at last the poison was gone out of him and the boy's whole body was being cleansed with new blood flowing from his lesions, I left their home, gasping for fresh air and thinking in horror and dismay, *I have never seen such foul results of sin as that! If this is the way to heal sick people–too much burden for me! What will happen to my future?* And I went straight to church to have overnight prayer with my faithful wife.

Later that same night, a radiant and handsome young man, the same son of that Baptist minister, came to the church. Weeping, he said to me, "Mister Kim, look at me! Until you came today to my father's house, I did not believe in Jesus. I hate poverty. My minister-father has always been so poor, I could not even go to school. I went away from him to the big city to make money for myself. But when I got this sickness, I came home to die. Then you came and showed me the love of God. Look at me now! Just in these few hours, I am completely healed. And I know that the God Who healed me will supply all my other needs, too. So now, I want to go to theological school to become minister of the Gospel like you. I believe in God, and I want only to bring glory to Him." I could hardly believe my eyes and ears at such a magnificent display of God's power and mercy.

Other desperate parents heard what had happened. A mother and father brought their paralyzed seven-year-old daughter to the church. My heart wept for her, so small, so pitiful. I prayed for her on the spot, and the child stood up, then she walked–the first miracle I had seen of a cripple raised. How faithful was God!

That night, in the spirit I saw hundreds of cripples lying in a row. Earnestly I wept and prayed over them all night long, "God, give me the power to heal all the sick and all the crippled."

Twelve

Raised From the Dead

Lazarus is dead...But let us go to him.
John 11:14b,15 NIV

July 1962: Kwang-si, Yesan

In Korea in those days, believers in Jesus were rare. Unbelievers persecuted them severely while watching them closely.

Meanwhile, an unhappy, young, technical high-school graduate named Chang, Byung Chan, moved down from Seoul to Kwang-si, where he began attending services at the Kwang-si Baptist Church. One Sunday morning, he stood solemnly in the church service singing the lyrics to the hymn-song written out on a poster board, when he was suddenly and supernaturally filled with a peace far beyond his scope of comprehension. Shortly after this transforming experience, he became a deacon of the church, and he and I soon became constant companions.

One afternoon in July 1962, a messenger from Chang informed me that twenty-four-year-old Deaconess Noh

Je Sook, a diligent worker at the Kwang-si Baptist Church, had succumbed three days earlier to an undiagnosed disease. The neighbors from that remote village, mostly unbelievers, had spent the two nights in the next room to bewail the dead and console the relatives. As Korean custom dictated, the body lay tightly bound by cords with the legs and arms straight down, both thumbs straight up and tied together, and the nostrils tightly plugged with cotton balls. Covered with a linen sheet, the body lay indoors on a low table behind a folding screen awaiting burial. Meanwhile, the lady's alcoholic husband argued heatedly with her very young Christian daughters over the type of funeral service to have for her that afternoon. He insisted that she had not been a member of the Christian church, but the daughters insisted that she most assuredly was. Many people were inside the house, where Deacon Chang kept watch over the body, but others were waiting out in the yard for Mister Kim (me) to come and settle the dispute.

As I prayed in the spirit during the twenty-minute walk up the hill from my house to her house, Scripture passages kept coming to my mind, specifically ones showing that, while on earth, Jesus apparently never considered a dead person irreversibly dead. He said of Lazarus, "He is asleep" (Jn. 11:11). He said to Jairus and his family, "Your daughter is sleeping" (Lk. 8:52). He said to the widow of Nain, "Don't cry!" Then He restored her dead son to her alive (Lk. 7:11-15).

At the top of the hill, I skirted around the people waiting outside for the burial, and went into the dark house to find Chang. Since electricity had not yet come to that area, the dim light inside came only from flickering candles and sputtering oil lamps. Chang told me that, all during the time he spent alone with the body behind the screen, he felt strangely uncomfortable as though in the presence of evil. Regardless, we knew the lady had been a Christian, and we decided to spend the night there in prayer, neither of us expecting anything out of the ordinary to happen.

As we prayed silently in the spirit, the same Scriptures kept coming back to my mind: *Lazarus is sleeping; daughter of Jairus is sleeping.* And in the middle of the night, I came to this conclusion: *Chang and I are here, and Jesus lives in us–our hope of glory. Therefore, Jesus is here. So, if Jesus is here, He will say the same thing of Deaconess Noh, that she is sleeping. If someone is sleeping, that person can wake up. Since that woman back there is only sleeping for these many hours, I will slap her face, and she will wake up.*

I told Chang what I knew I had to do. I also knew that if anyone besides Chang saw me doing it, there would be trouble. But when Chang and I stepped behind the screen, I went ahead anyway. After untying the cords from her thumbs, arms and legs, I opened the upper part of her clothing, grabbed her bare shoulders, and forced her body up into a sitting position. Chang and I were both startled to hear something snap and break in her mid-section. Regardless, I slapped her and shouted, "Wake up!"

Instantly, she flung herself forward. Her eyes and mouth flew open wide. The two cotton nose-plugs flew across the room, and she unburdened herself of a belly full of stale air with a long, loud belch, while Chang and I hurriedly pulled her clothes back into order.

In the eerie light, when the other people in the house saw the body that had been unquestionably dead for about twelve hours rise up, they were so startled, they almost fainted. They yelled and shouted and ran around in circles, rolled their eyes, waved their arms in the air, and rammed into each other.

After the initial shock, I reacted impulsively to the deeply ingrained, fearsome Korean proverb that warns, "When dead person sits up, knock body back down. If body hits you first, you die out." Fear surged through my entire system as I slapped her again, shouting to the dead spirit in her, "Come out! Come out!"

To my relief, she fell back. But then, a man's gravelly voice shouted back at me from out of her mouth, "I'm going!"

Startled by such a voice certainly not hers, I demanded to know, "Who are you?"

"I am Choi!"

"Choi is who? Who is Choi?"

The voice answered, "I am the spirit of Mr. Choi who died out a year ago from the poison spray on the farm."

Yes, I remembered: Local farmers had sprayed the insecticide DDT heavily across their rice fields, and many people died from inhaling it. But this dead farmer's voice was talking to me from the woman's mouth! I had read in the Bible about demons speaking that way, but I never imagined that I would have that kind of confrontation. I thought casting out demons only happened 2,000 years ago in Bible times. But now such a situation was facing me in real life. The demon inside of her body claimed to be the deceased Choi, and the only Scriptural thing I could think of to say–to shout–was, "Come out! Go into pigs!"

While I kept shouting and slapping the woman's face, the man's voice kept answering me, "I'm coming out! I'm coming out!" But he did not come out.

By then, the startled mourners were huddled together, closely watching what was happening. The believers were praying furiously; the unbelievers, staring like zombies.

When I asked the demon, "Why did you come into this lady?" he actually explained: While he, the wealthy bachelor-farmer Choi, was dying from the poison DDT, relatives of the lady's husband brought her to his home to care for him, and she had put a pillow under his head. Because she was kind to him, he decided that, after he died, he would "clothe himself in her tabernacle." Then the demon made an astonishing request of me: "Call my mother; call my brother to come here to speak with me through this lady's body."

I refused, but the news spread. Others ran and summoned Choi's elder brother, who in turn ran to town and, shamed by the report, demanded to know from the Baptist minister, "How come my dead brother got into the lady and speaks like that?" But the minister did not have an answer for him.

Soon, Choi's entire, humiliated family arrived, all especially ashamed that the man had died unmarried, and fearful that the situation would bring them bad luck of the worst kind–family ruin. His distraught mother kept asking, "Why are you doing this? You are dead. You are supposed to go far away. Why are you in this woman? Go away! You will bring bad luck."

At the same time, I had no idea how to deal with the situation, so I just kept on shouting at the spirit of the dead man to come out of her, and slapping her mouth until her jaw turned red. By this time Chang and the others had joined in the shouting and slapping.

When the demon tried to argue with me, I shouted, "Don't talk anymore! Come out!" Soon even the lady's husband came over and hit her face. When some of the young people saw that crazy scene, they confessed, "I also believe in Jesus! Let me do it!" and they joined in. Our intentions were the best; we just did not know the right thing to do.

The lady herself got up, stumbled around a little, tried to eat a little, and tried to sleep a little, at least when no one was slapping her. After being abused off and on for three whole days, she was bloody and exhausted, while the demon still refused to come out.

At that stage, I took time out to reason: *Jesus rebuked demons only once. It took Him no time at all to finish the job. Why, after three days, does this demon still not come out?*

I prayed earnestly about the matter until a certain aspect of one Scripture verse stood out in my mind, where Jesus drove out the demons by only one thing, His word (Mt. 8:16)! Greatly relieved, I finally understood that casting out demons was after all a very simple procedure, but we had to do it God's way. During those three days, we had continually tried to drive that demon out by hand.

I came back to the woman, and I spoke to the demon, "You unclean spirit, Jesus said to demons, 'You come out!' Jesus is here, and He says to you, 'Come out of her, and do not enter into her again!' "

The demon instantly replied, "Okay, I'm going." With that, the poor woman collapsed on the floor, and the demon left her.

That's when her young daughters began dancing around the yard and clapping their hands and praising God. Sadly, the unsaved husband was apparently unmoved, finding it impossible to deny old religious traditions by rejoicing in what God had done for his wife. But he said to his daughters, "I follow old tradition. You follow new tradition–go to Christian church, but I do not go with you." If his heart had not been softened somewhat, he never would have allowed that, for fear that, when he died, they would not show him continual honor and respect by taking food to his grave, as was their tradition, and he would consequently become a wandering, restless spirit out in the cold.

I was thrilled and honored that God would perform such a miracle through me. Chang, who had great natural leadership ability, agreed to join with me from that time on in a prayer ministry for healing the sick and casting out demons. We both knew then that we wanted to hold evangelistic crusades together.

As the news spread, my own Methodist pastor scheduled me to preach at the Yesan church. In spite of my unconquerable stutter, I stood in front of them and started preaching one night at 8 p.m. to forty people, and the Holy Spirit began moving among them. By the time I had preached for ten hours, 161 more people had come in to listen, and 160 of them were filled with the Holy Spirit, praising God, and speaking in tongues.

After that meeting, news of God's mighty miracles spread, and many churches all over the countryside invited me to come and preach for them. Remembering what the Lord taught me about prayer, I prayed all the time for the love of God and the power to heal, always making prayer my first priority. One deaconess, who heard me pray aloud, said, "Brother Kim seems to be storing up a great flood of saved-up prayer to God."

When I heard that, I thought, *Yes, that's what I want to do–keep making prayer-deposits in God's bank for use later on to bless the people.*

With my pastor's encouragement, every day I worked very hard to preach and to heal the sick, crazy to do God's work, always fervently praying, "Lord, give me the power to heal all the sick and all the crippled, and to cast out demons." I also prayed for two other things just as fervently–a son and a tent.

Thirteen

Serve God and Pastor

Yet he did not waver through unbelief regarding the promise of God, but was strengthened in his faith and gave glory to God, being fully persuaded that God had power to do what he had promised. Romans 4:20,21 NIV

...in whom he believed–the God who gives life to the dead and calls things that are not as though they were. Romans 4:17 NIV

August–December 1962: Yangkok, Yesan

The Yangkok Methodist Church in Chungnam Province was about a three-hour (90-mile) drive from Seoul. When the head-minister, Park Youngkil, who was visiting our area, heard me praying to God with great fervor, he invited me to lead a six-day crusade at his church from a Monday through Saturday. Still a lowly layman, I nevertheless accepted gladly, believing correctly that my own pastor would approve this breakthrough opportunity for me to lead my very first crusade, and to preach for the very first time from behind a pulpit.

In preparation, the Lord laid a Scripture upon my heart: "For whosoever will save his life shall lose it: and whosoever will lose his life for my sake shall find it" (Mt. 16:25). I determined then not to care for my own life, but to be only His voice during those six services.

Meanwhile, Chang confided to me that the shock of seeing the dead woman raised up in Kwang-si, cripples walking unaided, the sick healed, lepers cleansed, and demons cast out, had led him into a deeper study of the Bible as the living Word of God. Throughout our ministering together, he checked continually to see if we were doing the right thing according to the Bible. We were, and countless miracles became our daily norm. Therefore, we reconfirmed our agreement to stick together, holding evangelistic crusades wherever the Lord would lead us. Chang would be in charge of organizing the details; I would be the evangelist.

Arriving at the Yangkok Methodist Church, we approached the place and the day with great expectations. But right away I noticed two disheartening details: the neglected condition of the church property, and, even worse, the marks of prolonged malnutrition on the drawn faces of the pastor and his family, and their pathetic living conditions.

Pastor Park's situation, however, was not unique. Almost all the rural pastors in Korea at that time suffered dire poverty along with their doleful memories of Japanese rule. It was they who had been sought out for persecution, imprisonment, torture, and death. During the Korean War, the same. Even nine years after that war had ended, still almost no one wanted to become a minister, especially the sons of ministers, who understandably did not want to live in want like their fathers. And no minister in Korea, except the tenacious few, wanted to devote his son to that kind of life, even though some lay-Christians regarded a pastor's suffering as his opportunity "to develop a godly character."

Pastor Park's thirty-member congregation supported him with a tight fist, even though on his part he was honest, godly and generous, freely sharing the little he had with others in need. Unseen by my host, I opened the lid to his rice jar and discovered that it contained not one grain of rice. Granted, money was scarce, and the church members often shared their rice with him, but rice did not clothe his family. I thought, *If Jesus were here, He would change this situation.*

Deacon Chang and I put our things down in the church, set up my new blackboard at the front of the sanctuary, and then went outside to put up posters, distribute handbills, and parade through the streets Korean-style, singing and beating our drum, thus summoning the neighbors to the revival-crusade. The chief aim of such meetings was to take the Gospel to unbelievers who, we hoped, would be brought by their Christian family or friends.

That evening, about forty people, half of them unbelievers from the town, gathered at the church for the first service. After privately, humbly surrendering my stutter to the Lord, I stood up to preach at 8:30 p.m., centering my sermon on the probing question, "How much grace have you received?"

Using colored chalk I illustrated my message on a blackboard for the first time. I sketched the Old Testament Tabernacle in the Wilderness–the layout and floor plan, the furniture, the coverings, the complete design and all the appointments, as detailed in Exodus 25–30, showing how altogether they comprise a blueprint for holy, Christian living, and how perfectly they reflect the riches of God's grace towards us through our Lord and Savior, Jesus Christ.

I preached all night until six o'clock in the morning. In spite of my stutter, which persisted in hammering out some of my words in repetitions, no one shifted, no one squirmed, but all sat quietly and still, as though enraptured by God's Word. No one moved from his place.

On the second night, a hundred more from the village crowded in among the members of the congregation. Again I preached on the Tabernacle, developing the message further. But during that night, unruly youth from the neighborhood, accustomed to persecuting that particular church, stood outside the open window, laughing at my stammer, shouting, and interrupting me.

On the third night, one of them hurled a stone through the window, aimed straight at my face. To everyone's astonishment including my own, as the stone flew in my direction, it suddenly ricocheted as though it had bounced off an invisible, solid wall.

Gasps and cries exploded from the congregation inside, while the youth outside stood at the window stunned into silence. Together Pastor Park and I rushed outside. The culprits stared at me in terror, but Pastor Park herded them into the church, where I made them sit down, pray to God for forgiveness, and pay attention to the rest of my sermon. Only God knows how many of them were redirected from lives of crime by that miracle, but most of those boys came back to hear more about Jesus the next day. So many other villagers, who heard the report about the deflected stone, showed up on the fourth day, that not one square-inch of space on the floor was left unoccupied.

Humbly grateful for God's intervention and anointing, I still grieved over the pastor's dreadful living conditions, and on the sixth and final night, I challenged the senior elders and deacons to stand up and state publicly how much salary they paid their pastor. They humbly confessed to a meager two dollars a week.

Forcefully, urgently, and without apology, I made my appeal to them and to the other members: "The unbelieving world cannot see God, but they are able to see the works of those claiming to be God's people. Unbelievers in your village and round about are not receiving very good messages about the love of God for His people because of your lack of care for your pastor. Since you have received the grace of God all this week, begin to treat your pastor right. I challenge you to give him twenty dollars every month. Double his amount of rice! Make him a new suit! Serve God, but also serve your pastor! He is worthy of your support."

Along with my appeal came the gentle Holy Spirit's conviction to their hearts, and the church rose to the challenge: They agreed to raise Pastor Park's salary immediately. Someone in the group volunteered to make a dress for his wife; another, to replace the pastor's make-shift, rubber slippers with real shoes; someone else, to provide clothes for their children so they could begin attending school. They also promised to cover all the basic needs of the family, and all those pledges were kept.

At the close of the crusade, another pastor invited me to preach the following weekend at his church, and once again I gladly accepted–my second such open door. This time I would illustrate through the details of the Tabernacle how well the priests and high priests of God lived under His provision for them through the tithes and offerings of His people. Again, I could repeat my challenge to take better care of the pastor, and I determined to lead a general campaign to inspire all Korean church congregations to support their pastors well. I gave the same challenge in every church: "Look at how your pastor has to live! You can treat him better than this."

Pastors heard, and invitations came from all over South Korea, in number far exceeding the possibility of my responding to them all. I visited over a thousand churches, often leading as many as three evangelistic services a day, and in every church, the same plea. I cried out against the poverty of church workers, against the neglect of Bible study, against the practice of unscriptural doctrines and rituals, against leaders lording it over their congregations, but mainly against poverty. Eventually, I even dared to suggest that some congregations buy their pastors automobiles.

On the whole, as soon as congregations began treating their pastors better, the pastors showed more enthusiasm for working with their people, and the congregations in turn made improvements to the church property. Then, because of a dramatic increase in their membership, hundreds of churches built new sanctuaries, and I became widely known as the evangelist who turns churches upside down.

Predictably, some of the older evangelists did not like this. Too many people stopped following their crusades to go where God was working miracles. Too, my purely biblical message created unrest among pastors of some of the smaller churches who were content to maintain their existing size. When their criticism against me turned into shouting even while I was preaching, branding me heretic and sheep stealer, I renewed my decision to keep a pebble in my mouth as a reminder never to criticize, especially from the pulpit, but only to preach the Gospel, and to pray for the needs of the people.

"What's the matter with you?" some of the people demanded of me. "Why don't you answer them back? Why don't you shut them up? You see, but you don't talk!" And they gave me the nickname, *Semone* (the "mute").

It then became my habit, after each time of preaching, to go outside alone to find another pebble, to help me live up to my nickname, Semone: "I see, but I keep silent."

Soon, news of God's powerful miracles was spread abroad throughout the countryside, and invitations came from even more pastors for me to deliver God's Word in their churches.

By December 1962, several groups of Christians had asked me to pastor their pastorless churches, but I declined. I had no intention of launching a new congregation with members who had left other churches. But my own pastor, Kyung Lin Oh, strongly encouraged me in that direction, believing that I could be an effective pastor. I considered his words prayerfully, while still believing my call was to evangelism. Having not been to any seminary, I was not even a deacon; certainly I was not qualified to pastor a church. I only knew that I was called by God to lead miracle crusades.

Fourteen

No Man's Debtor

Am I now trying to win the approval of men, or of God? Or am I trying to please men? If I were still trying to please men, I would not be a servant of Christ. Galatians 1:10 NIV

January–June 1963: Kwang-si, Pibong, Chungbang Mountain

Kang Soon and I had known for several months that we were going to be blessed with a child, and in spite of our personal poverty, I prayed like this every day: "I say very honestly to You, God, if You give me a son, I will give him back to You." I prayed like that in spite of my wife's mixed feelings. She considered my prayer somewhat akin to Abraham's giving his son Isaac up to God—even more difficult than giving oneself.

In February, my wife, who never in her life had eaten well but concerned herself only with my health, was nearing the end of her pregnancy and feeling a little uneasy about her diet. Since we had been unable to afford meat for about eight months, we agreed that she should go to the marketplace and buy a little beef or pork, then prepare a special breakfast for just the two of us. She went, then made a delicious pork-and-cabbage stew with the usual side dishes of rice, kimchee, and seaweed, then set the meal on a little, low side table small enough to make the food look more abundant. Then we prayed over it, dedicating ourselves to live by all possible means in accordance with the Lord's will.

At the end of our prayer, quite unexpectedly a shabbily dressed old woman, one we had never seen before, squeezed herself through the very narrow passageway alongside our kitchen stove and into our room. She shuffled over to the table, sat down on a floor cushion, and asked for food.

I looked at Kang Soon and she looked at me. Then we remembered the same Scripture at the same time, that Jesus said, "Do not refuse anything to anyone who asks" (Mt. 5:42). So, we placed our meal before the beggar.

While she ate, I prayed. Then she asked for money. I had only ten *won* (800 won = $1/US) tucked away in my Bible, but I gave her all I had. She took it, then shuffled out the same way she had come in. While we watched, she disappeared. We ran outside to see where she would go next, but she was nowhere. We questioned a teenager nearby, who said he had seen no one leave.

Greatly puzzled, we went back into our room, sank to our knees, and prayed. As we asked God for clear understanding, He graciously gave both of us visions: In mine I saw a clear light flowing into our room from the north side and exiting towards the south. Kang Soon envisioned an angel of God sitting at our table eating our meal, taking our money, and leaving. Amazed, we hastened to the church, and there described the woman, what she had done, and our visions to the other lay-persons there, who then came to our room, sang hymn-songs of praise to God with us for awhile, then prayed with us again. They listened to our testimony over and over, wondering what it could mean. All that came to my mind was that God is no man's debtor.

Early the following morning, we were visited by five irate laymen from the small Pibong Methodist Church about three miles away. They were a hostile group who up to that time had unanimously, vocally and violently opposed my personal ministry. Ironically, a local minister, whom they had invited to preach for them that same night, had canceled. After some private and heated discussion among themselves, the laymen finally, reluctantly consented to ask me to come in his place. I accepted without hesitation.

In the late afternoon, Kang Soon and I went down to the church in Pibong, and were astounded when we saw the food prepared for us–the very same dishes we served to the stranger the day before, but more, so much more of everything.

At the night service, the few people who came were deeply moved by my sermon from the Bible. All were blessed and healed and filled with the Holy Spirit, so much so that the senior pastor, who was leaving for another church, asked me to take over his pastorate. Surprised by his request, I firmly declined. I was not authorized by the Methodist denomination to pastor a church. But he was so insistent, I finally agreed to go with him to discuss it with the Supervisor of the Regional Methodist Association. To my amazement, the Supervisor ordered me to assume responsibility for that frail, little five-year-old congregation with fewer than ten members. I thought, *Well, I don't seem to have any choice here!*

In early March, we moved from Kwang-si down to Pibong into our first parsonage, one small room attached to the church, which itself was just a dirty, decrepit, ramshackle old farmhouse–not a good place to take a very pregnant wife. When I peered down through a hole in the kitchen floor, directly beneath my gaze I saw three weathered, wooden coffins, and a few neglected grave markers. Evidently, known only to the church deacons, our quarters had been built over a graveyard. I did not inform my wife.

On March 17, I was commissioned lay-minister at Pibong Methodist Church. That was how and where I first became a pastor.

On the very next day, March 18, the first of two momentous events occurred in our lives: While wearing my one-and-only, itchy, rumpled, black suit with its sweat-streaked collar, I presided over my first church service as a pastor, with Kang Soon, Deacon Chang, my mother and me making up half the congregation.

The second momentous event occurred the next day: Kang Soon endured natural childbirth to bring forth our beautiful son, Sung Hyun. God had answered my prayer.

By then, I had been praying for a tent for four years. My heart was set on conducting crusade-meetings in a tent, even though South Korea weather clearly limits the time for such meetings from early April, when monsoon season begins, to late September or early October. The rest of the year is too cold.

Convinced that there was no better way than through tent ministry to reach unbelievers who would not cross the threshold of a church but, at the same time, were not intimidated by going into a tent, I was also convinced that there was no better way to encourage believers than by proving God's presence among them through Christ's holy miracles. In my heart I longed to demonstrate to all my hurting countrymen that God Himself was not too proud, too serene, nor too unapproachable to show up at a lowly tent meeting in order to bless them. Chang and I, therefore, set up our Evangelistic Healing Crusade Team, and continued to pray.

The next month, God granted my four-year-long prayer request for a tent, when one of my church members lent me a tent big enough for 150 people, one that had been used in the factory where he worked. Thrilled and excited, Chang and I immediately began to equip the tent. And, even though monsoon season was upon us, we scheduled a week-long, revival tent-crusade about three miles from Yesan in a thick forest up Chungbang Mountain. And, since Chungbang Mountain was an area famous for its toxic pine caterpillars, other bothersome insects, poisonous vipers, and all kinds of worms squirming around on the ground, Chang and I began praying for protection from the nasty "creepy-crawlers," as well as for the rains to hold off. We also began advertising in earnest by putting up our posters, passing out handbills, and beating our drum in the streets.

As soon as we started packing up the tent, the loudspeakers, and the food for the week-long crusade, some of the church members came to warn me: "Pastor, you won't have any crusade-meeting on top of the mountain. It's time for monsoon. It will rain so hard, nobody will come."

"Well," I said, "we have the food prepared and the tent and everything else for the meetings, and we prayed a lot about it to God, so now we have to do it."

Early in the morning, the rain sheeted down like a waterfall. When we started up the mountain, it stopped. We had clear skies all the way to the top. When the volunteers had the 150-capacity tent up, I took a head count: Exactly 150 people had gathered together on the mountain for the evangelistic meetings. After the count, nobody else came.

I called everyone together, to pray and rebuke the caterpillars, pesky bugs, snakes, worms—all things evil—and tell them in no uncertain terms in Jesus' name to leave us alone. Whenever the dark clouds gathered over us and big rain drops threatened to slap down on us, we spoke to the rain: "Rain, you go away from this place!" When it thundered, we shouted, "You thunderclouds and lightning, leave us alone!"

Suddenly, a hole in the black, storm-cloud canopy opened up over us, a big hole through which we saw the calm blue sky. The hole stayed directly over our camp throughout the entire week, while the downpour surrounded us like a circular waterfall. We watched the water flooding down into the valley, and I suddenly understood why more people had not come: Even while we remained dry, it rained so hard down in the village, nobody dared venture outside.

In spite of the obvious miracle, one of our other layministers said to the others, "Well, sooner or later we'll be hit by the rain, so let's be prepared for it." As soon as some of them started digging a ditch to divert the anticipated flood away from the tent, a sudden screaming wind ripped into the tent, sliced the top open, and scared us almost out of our wits.

I fell to my knees, beseeching God for mercy while rocking back and forth, back and forth, confessing aloud that only God Himself could redeem our situation and bless these courageous people through such a powerless leader as I.

Since there was nothing else we could do, we convened for first the evening service under the ripped tent. First, we prayed and praised and sang to God. Then, using the Bible as my only text, I shouted over the racket of the rain with my scratchy, hoarse voice, comparing spiritual truth with spiritual truth (1 Cor. 2:13).

God confirmed His presence with us by performing many, many miracles during the night, spontaneously healing the people of their diseases as they listened to His servant and believed His promises:

A paralyzed blind woman, who had been carried up piggy-back by her granddaughter, suddenly leapt to her feet and danced for joy before the Lord. She could not only dance; she could see!

A man, who had knelt down to pray, jumped up and testified that he had just crushed two poisonous vipers under his knees.

A leprous girl, who lived just down the road, shouted to us that the red spots on her face had disappeared, and that her sense of touch had been restored.

Two leprous men, who had climbed up the mountainside with us, professed to being miraculously healed during the praise and worship.

Many others claimed the greatest miracle of all–changed outlooks, changed lives, changed destinies–by asking Jesus Christ to become their Savior and Lord.

Of the 150 people who came, 120 of them asked to be baptized by immersion in Jesus' name as soon as possible, even though it was against Methodist policy to baptize in that manner.

On the seventh day, which dawned clear and cloudless, we realized other miracles had happened during the week: No ants had found their way into our food, nobody had been stung or bitten by insects, and the snakes slithering all around us had harmed no one. And until we descended the mountain, we did not realize the destructive force of the deluge–roads were washed out, trees and buildings toppled, people's possessions swept away by mud slides. But our surprise was nothing compared to the villagers' amazement in seeing us coming safely down.

"How was it possible for you to stay up there on the mountain the whole week?" they asked us. "We have not seen one day since you left without a devastating downpour. We thought all you Jesus freaks had perished in the storm."

Once home, we patched and returned the tent. Then, as pastor of the Pibong Methodist Church, I invited Kim, Chung Ki, pastor of the Hahm Yul Baptist Church, to come to Pibong and hold a revival. After a time of fruitful ministry, that visiting Baptist pastor baptized 116 of the people who had asked for immersion–a definite violation of Methodist policy.

When the Methodist Denominational Board heard about it and wanted to place blame for the "rudeness" on the visiting Pastor Kim, I quickly immersed four members of the church in order to assume full responsibility and all blame to myself. As a result, I was promptly, but only temporarily, removed from service and summoned to a hearing before the District Methodist Court by the church authorities, who were only acting in accordance with their denominational guidelines. The hearing came to nothing, but their opposition to my biblical, Holy Ghost practices continued to intensify. By the time their arbitrary contravention died down, I had been summoned to trial six times. (I remain guilty as charged.)

During the first week in May, we borrowed another tent–a heavy, ugly, bulky military tent that could hold 300 people. It had two tall metal center posts, sixty shorter posts around the circumference, and eight more to reinforce the entrance.

Chang and I tied the tent and all seventy posts into four big bundles, then wrapped the loudspeakers, the battery, the posters, the drum, and our personal effects into six more bundles—ten big bundles altogether. We piled some of the bundles onto a two-wheeled cart, and the rest we packed on wooden H-shaped frames, which we strapped to our backs. Then we set out to conduct a tent crusade in Taesul-Myun on Chungbang Mountain about twenty minutes from Yesan, pushing the cart and walking the entire distance between Pibong and the Seoul train station, to ship them south from there on the Southwest Railroad.

Not until we arrived at the train station, hot, sweaty and exhausted, did I remember that I was broke. So was Chang. I left him at the ticket office guarding our pile of baggage, and headed out towards a relative's house twelve miles away, covering part of the distance by streetcar, then running the rest of the way. I borrowed just enough money for two tickets, and started back. Hoarding every precious won, I rode part of the way back, then got out and ran again because the streetcar was too slow. I arrived just in time to board the train.

At the end of the line, we still had five miles to go by bus, still had ten big bundles to carry, still had no money–not for bus fares or food or anything else–and had not eaten all day. It was time for prayer.

As soon as we knelt down in the middle of the train-station waiting room, two young men wearing big smiles ran over to welcome us. They lugged all our bundles to the bus depot and loaded them onto the bus which had just pulled in. When we boarded, I quietly confessed to the ticket taker, "Lady, I have no m-m-m-money for f-f-fares."

"Oh," she said, "they're already paid for. That man back there..." She indicated a man already seated. I recognized him from an earlier crusade when I laid hands on him and prayed for his healing from inflammation of his joints. The man had been healed suddenly several months later while working on his farm, and was on his way to our crusade.

The first night, I preached to about 700 people; some crowded into the tent, and others gathered outside. I spoke on the works of Christ being the same today as they were when He walked the earth. After the sermon, I called the sick to stand up. Almost all of the people stood to their feet. I told them to place their own hands on their afflicted areas, close their eyes, and we would all pray together. First, I led them in earnest prayer. Then, moving in the supernatural gift of the word of knowledge, I called out the diseases one by one, and the Spirit of God moved among them and healed their bodies. When I asked those who had just been healed to come forward and tell about it, so many lined up to testify that it took well over an hour to hear them all.

So many were healed on the first day that, on the second day, there were only about ten percent still sick. On the third day, when I cast out demons, the people screamed and cried and wept and sobbed, but afterwards, there was great rejoicing with a huge pile of crutches thrown away by formerly "incurable" paralytics.

One man, who had two hard lumps in his stomach the size of his fists, suffered such excruciating pain that he was not able to eat without vomiting. When demons were cast out of him, he fell to the ground and writhed in agony, but when he stood back up to his feet, tears of joy were streaming down his cheeks as he testified that all the pain had gone and the lumps were also gone. To celebrate, someone gave him some solid food, which he ate with comfort and joy.

One man, whose joints were so painfully inflamed that he had not been able to bend his fingers or knees or ankles for over six years, was instantly healed, and he jumped up and down, leaping and praising God. The next day with all his fingers, toes and other joints completely normal, he began helping with the hard, physical labor at the crusade–without pain.

I stayed so busy healing the sick and preaching, I hardly had time to buy even a little boiled rice at the edge of the market for my one and only meal a day. Almost starving, I survived mainly on joy from seeing so many signs and wonders and miracles of salvation.

One night inside the tent, I saw the Lord Himself kneeling down as though praying over our improvised pulpit, and I remembered His words: "*...go...teaching them to obey everything I have commanded you. And surely I am with you always, to the very end of the age*" (Mt. 28:19,20 NIV).

His command, to teach both the new Christians and all who were healed to grow in their faith after we left, became a heavy, heavy burden to me. So during the afternoons, I began instructing the people that they must obey His Word, that their spiritual lives must line up with the Bible. I specifically emphasized that the Lord's words are eternally the same. In light of that teaching, I made them promise me that those who believed the Word would lay hands on the sick and pray for their healing, and begin doing it the very first day after they returned home.

Fifteen

Ultimate Poverty

May those who hope in you not be disgraced because of me, O Lord, the Lord Almighty; may those who seek you not be put to shame because of me, O God of Israel. Psalm 69:6 NIV

June–September 1963: Pibong, Young Moon Mountain, Pibong

It is Korean custom to consider a newborn baby to be one year old at birth. It is also Korean custom to celebrate the infant's 100th day: If one survived the first 100 days, he had a good chance to survive the entire first year. On June 25, therefore, I celebrated my son Sung Hyun's 100th day by going to church with his mother to pray, and on that special day I prayed my usual prayer devoting him to God.

In Korea at that time, the most open-minded statement that could be expected from a devoted but poor minister-father would be, "I want my son to be medical doctor or a college professor, but if he decides for himself to become a minister instead, I will let him."

By the middle of July, I had pastored the Pibong Church for four months, long enough for me to know beyond any doubt, despite the 180 people then attending regularly, that I personally lacked all things necessary for being a good pastor, especially prayer and humility. I was not looking for more ability to minister, but to pursue my conviction that only after I died, could Jesus' love flow from me to others. I knew that in my own strength I could do nothing, but that with God all things are possible. I felt such an urgency to have another forty days of fasting-prayer to seek God's help and direction, that I told my wife what I had to do, and I left the church in her care. She considered herself a weak woman, but I knew better than that.

On July 10, I traveled the four hours up to Young Moon Mountain to be alone with God. In that mountainous area are several *chons,* or villages. I rented a room at Mit-eum Chon, or Faith Village, and while there wrote down three specific subjects for my prayer focus during my fast: 1) for my fleshly passions to disappear from my mind, 2) for me to be His powerful servant in every way, and 3) for me to always have His power to heal the sick.

I went up into the mountain to find a secluded place. I had no other desire at the time, except that somehow in some way, my ego had to die. That was my determination.

For the first ten days, even though I drank a little water, it was hard to endure the hunger. Then the hunger passed. During the next ten days, I continued taking water, but soon realized that the water made me weak. Remembering from the Bible that on two occasions Moses fasted for forty days without water encouraged me, so for the rest of the time, I did not even drink water.

Even though I did not see anyone during the first twelve days, I could hear voices and movement in the woods. On the twelfth day, I moved deeper into the woods to a more secluded place to be absolutely alone with God.

There I discovered that hunger is not the most unendurable circumstance for man: Loneliness is. Man can go without food, go without water, go without shoes, without clothes, without shelter, but man cannot go without human companionship. We cannot survive ultimate loneliness because loneliness is the ultimate poverty.

Even though I prayed aloud through three days and three nights without rest, the solitude, the not seeing any other living soul, was the most painful fast.

Somehow, I endured the forty days, realizing beyond any doubt the immutable fact that a human being is a creature not made to live alone.

Through that revelation I determined this before God: "I will love even the lonely leper. I will love all the unlovely, lonely, disabled people, whoever they may be, whatever their disability, whatever their disease. I will love them because they are not lowly creatures on their way to becoming oxen or dogs or worms or other dumb animals, as Buddhists believe, but they are immortal human beings made in Your image and Your likeness, on their way into eternity." And I saw then that my three prayer subjects were merely three aspects of one progressive prayer, that my flesh should give way to serving His people in His power.

In early September, I returned home bony, haggard, unkempt, and pale, but with renewed and deep appreciation for my devoted wife, my steadfast friend Chang, and the faithful members of my little church. So intense was my desire for continual close communion with God, that I was only partially aware of having become a mere skeleton of a man. Only by God's abundant mercy and grace did I recuperate fully in only a few days.

Then, when I realized my beloved Kang Soon was distraught, I called her to me, and said, "Come here, wife, and tell me what is on your mind."

"My husband, I am weak woman..."

"Yes, yes, I know all about that."

"...and I need you to pray for me."

"Well, what about? Tell me what is wrong."

Kang Soon sat down and folded her hands in her lap, then began speaking. "Well, it goes back for some time. First time I saw demon cast out, fear came to my mind, especially at night I remembered. I know demons shout and cry and insane persons go wild, but then when demons go out, person comes back to normal. I don't like seeing that, hearing how person express himself at that time.

"You know, Yuhbo, I depend on God and pray a lot for His help. When you left me in charge of church this time, a family called me to their home, and sick person was there sitting in front of me. While I was singing to him, person's eyes became wide open, so I was afraid of looking at his eyes. I sang louder, and his mouth started opening, and he showed strange face to me. I was nervous inside, so I pray for him, sing a few songs, read Bible to him, then I come home.

"Even after I returned home, I didn't feel right that I had failed in my first visitation. When I tried to pray to God, I saw that man's eyes in my vision, so I could not pray. I tried again, and his mouth showed, so I could not concentrate on prayer. I thought, when Yuhbo comes home, he will pray for me, and I will feel all right inside, have peace of mind. So, now you pray?"

"What?" I said in surprise. "You are a soldier! When you visit that kind of family, you go to fight with the enemy. You should have prepared. You must always pray for God's intention before you go on visitation. As pastor's wife, your role is not to follow pastor all the time. You have to be partner, minister in your own right, prepared in every way. You are clean person, Kang Soon, but when you go into ministry, all kinds of people come—dirty persons, all kinds of seriously diseased persons—because they hear that, if they come to me, they will be healed. So, when I am away from home, you have to take care of those sick people. You have to practice your own ministry, do what is in the Bible, what you have learned from watching me. Don't be afraid, my wife. It is not you who will do the work; it is God, but you have to go prepared."

She thought a minute, then nodded her head. "Then I want to study," she said.

I nodded too, satisfied. "Yes, you will. And so will I."

Not long after that, a mother brought her crippled seven-year-old daughter to me. Discerning God's intention, I took the child's hand and pulled her up to her feet, then told her mother to call her name. She called, I took my hands away, and for the first time in her life the child walked to her mother—a miracle of God.

I prayed for a middle-aged man with a hideous tumor growing on his chin. As soon as I touched it, the tumor shrank into nothing under my hand.

After that, so many miracles of healing and deliverance took place, we soon lost count once again.

A leper, who had been hiding in a cave, came to me privately for prayer. He was married and the father of a newborn daughter, but he could only see his wife and child from a distance. The poor man was terrified of being caught by the government and isolated with other lepers on a small island. The old scars on his face told me that, at one time, he had begun to heal.

"What is your name?" I asked him.

"It doesn't matter," he said sadly.

"It matters to me. What is your name?"

He muttered, "Lee" (not his real name). When I told him he needed to believe in Jesus, he screamed, "No, I don't want to!"

Then I asked him, "Mister Lee, are you leper?"

"No! I am not!" he shouted at me. "I have some other disease."

But I said, "Look at you. You have no eyebrows; your fingers are clawed; your sores are open. Nobody wants to come near you. People run away from you because you are leper. But I am not running away. I am coming to you for only one reason, to introduce you to Jesus. To prove it, I want to help you out by healing you of your leprosy. I want you to be saved. Do you believe me?"

He groaned. "What difference does it make whether I believe you, or whether I'm leper or not? I'm going to die from this disease anyway. I'll never again be able to love my wife or even to hug my child."

When I saw his defenses finally fall, I went to him, and embraced him. Then he submitted to me and let me do what the Lord had prompted me to do in Jesus' name–suck the poison out of his sores. Afterwards, I said to him, "After experiencing this from me, still you don't believe in Jesus?"

Weeping, he said, "I don't know." But a few days later, Lee came back to me publicly. His eyebrows had grown back and his fingers were returning to normal. He was healed. From then on, I took this normal, healthy person with me wherever I led crusades. And Lee soon began serving faithfully and enthusiastically with Preacher Chang and me on the Evangelistic Healing Crusade Team, praying for the sick and seeing them healed, and serving in the church.

From then on, crowds of people began coming to me to pray for their healing or for the healing of their friends. Whenever I prayed for the sick and lonely people, this was (and still is) my attitude: "God, please heal this person. If he is to die of this disease, let me take it to myself." I knew that only Jesus Himself can bear the infirmities of others, but I felt as though this prayer had come from God's heart. And in all those cases, when my heart is pure towards Him, no disease is contagious to me.

Sixteen

Beyond Exaggeration

"...No one who puts his hand to the plow and looks back is fit for service in the kingdom of God."
Luke 9:62 NIV

November 1963–February 1964: Pibong

Every day, wherever Chang and I went, we experienced such a dramatic flow of God's healing and restorative powers, we had no time to be overwhelmed by the magnitude of what He was accomplishing through the ministry. God showed Himself to be so great, so glorious, so powerful, so all-wise, that He was and is forever far beyond all exaggeration.

By November, Chang was an ordained lay-minister, one with the vision to take care of our church finances, Sunday school, and whatever else needed to be done. Chang did it all, leaving his home on his father's farm in the deep valley every day by 3 a.m., attending 4 a.m. prayer in Pibong, taking care of church business, then returning home late at night to help his father. He and

I prayed much together for God to use us to help the people. As a result, we saw so many miracles every day, we could not keep up with the numbers, names and places.

At the same time, we were still branded as heretics by many Christians, who denounced us specifically for casting out demons, which was not general practice in their own churches, and, therefore, considered by them to be "unscriptural." Sadly, most churches thereabouts focused exclusively on a few favorite passages of Scripture, using the same ones over and over, but neglecting the rest. While not desiring to hear directly from God through praying fervently in the spirit, nor searching the Scriptures daily to learn His ways, they were also not expecting to experience signs and miracles among themselves. Since we openly accepted the Bible from cover to cover as one complete and continuous revelation, and often prayed in tongues, we were targets of their criticism.

Disregarding their attacks, we continued to believe God and amazing things happened. I saw full well that miracles do not save souls: They simply advertise that Jesus Christ is alive and performing the same works today as He did on earth long ago.

As reports of Deaconess Noh's experience of being raised from the dead continued to spread throughout the countryside, it seemed that all hopeless cases were brought to me. Even when people died in the hospitals, relatives and friends brought the corpses to me in hopes that I would raise them up. I felt uncomfortable about this, knowing that God does not always heal. But, I reasoned, even though Jesus Himself raised only a few people from the dead, He raised some. It had happened in the Bible, so I tried to revive every dead body brought to me. The outcome, however, was always God's responsibility. If it was ever my fault because I had been lax or negligent in prayer, only God knew.

One who was not raised up was a twenty-two-year-old lady bank clerk. When she died, her mother insisted that I go to her home. The body was laid out in a room which had a clear-glass window in the bottom of the door. As I prayed fervently and honestly for a miracle of God, I became distracted by a blur of curious, eager eyes at that low window watching me. Losing my concentration, I became discouraged with the prayer, remembering that even Jesus Himself often had to be alone to pray. For whatever reason, sad to say, that woman did not revive.

During that time, so much was happening–so many people receiving prayer–that I was often unaware of the results of my prayers unless I was later informed.

We held a crusade-meeting, in February 1964, in the old army tent. Soon after the first morning service, when all the people had settled down on mats to share breakfast with their families, a painfully deformed woman was carried in and laid among them on a thick, soft cushion on the floor. Her bent knees had been locked and frozen in such a grotesque position for so long that the skin between her thighs and calves had grown together behind her knees like tough leather.

After calling the other Christians together to pray for God's mercy on the pitiful little lady, Chang and I asked God to show us His intention in the situation, and what we should do about her contorted legs.

You straighten them out.

How?

Force them out.

In obedience, we rebuked the demon that had her bound, then each of us took hold of one leg and knee, and pushed and pulled. The woman screamed, convulsing in agony. The strange skin began to tear and dark occult blood began to flow. Prompted by the Holy Spirit, Chang and I did not let up, but worked together, holding her down and forcing her frozen knee joints to unlock and straighten out. The scene was so heartrending, the stench so nauseating, that the other people gave up trying to eat; instead, they prayed with us louder and louder, many of them weeping and wailing over the poor woman shrieking in terror, while the reeking, rancid blood dripped down from her torn skin and soaked into the cushion.

Suddenly, the thought hit me, *If this lady is not healed, I could be arrested! Not Chang, though, because he's ordained. But I'm not even a deacon. If I'm going to keep on with this kind of ministry, I better go to seminary!*

Meanwhile, the terrified woman, who was almost fainting from the horror of her experience, kept pleading with us to stop, but we continued working on her legs, believing that what we had started, we had better finish.

Pretending to ignore the woman's frantic pleas to stop hurting her, to leave her as she was when she was first brought in, we nevertheless continued working with her legs for twenty minutes more. When the bands of skin behind her knees were finally torn apart, I commanded her in Jesus' name to stand up. Amazed, she was able to balance perfectly on her two feet for the first time ever, and even to walk. Every one of us wept. We all stood to our feet, raised our hands, clapped, shouted, and praised the Lord Who alone does such wondrous works.

Seventeen

His Servants' Words

The secret things belong to the Lord our God, but the things revealed belong to us....
Deuteronomy 29:29 NIV

March–May 1964: Pibong, Seoul

On March 17, my wife, my son, and I along with my mother and my brother moved into a rented room by the gate of a house. The room, only seven feet wide by seven feet long, was so small that no more than three adults could lie down at one time, so we had to sleep in shifts.

On March 18, we celebrated Sung Hyun's first birthday (two years old, Korean age) with a simple ceremony once again offering him to God for His service. By that time, my very sensitive and bright young son was already walking, and shortly thereafter, he caused us to have a miserable few hours when he wandered away from home. We searched frantically from early morning till three o'clock in the afternoon, at which time he suddenly reappeared, climbing back up our hill.

Without a doubt, God our Father had accepted him at his 100th-day dedication ceremony, and now his guardian angel had kept him from harm, for which we are humbly grateful.

During this time, Kang Soon, knowing my heart, decided that she herself would sew me a tent, a lightweight tent the same size as the army tent, one that would also hold 300 people. She amazed me by undertaking this task, since she already went out to work as a dental technician during the day, while my mother took care of our son. Not only that, but Kang Soon was willing to sew that huge tent in our tiny seven-foot square home. She borrowed money from our landlady, bought lengths of cotton cloth, and worked very hard at making me the best present I could receive. Meanwhile, I continued to dream and pray for a tent that would hold ten times that number.

During those months, wherever Chang and I went, we hauled the heavy army tent with us and did all the work of setting it up ourselves–Chang and I and Lee, the restored leper. Others helped sometimes, but mostly we three worked alone.

In April, we moved the tent down to Cheonan to hold a crusade. Again, my teaching was on how the Holy Place in the Tabernacle in the Wilderness discloses the Lord Jesus Christ. So many people crowded into the tent that I had to stand tight up against a corner. I began teaching and preaching at 4 a.m., and I kept speaking all day without a break. Nobody shifted; nobody moved except several who stood to their feet rejoicing when healed without any prayer or laying on of hands, but simply by believing the Word. When I finally came to the close of the service at 9:40 p.m., I realized that I had spoken to them continuously for seventeen hours and ten minutes, the longest I would ever preach, and the very first time without stuttering at all. Without drama or fanfare, the Lord had delivered me from my lifelong affliction.

From then on, every time I preached on the Tabernacle, I could hear the sound of the Lord's waterfall of love pouring out His healing upon the people, as we witnessed His wondrous works among them.

At one open-air meeting in late April, a middle-aged woman with a deformed hip was brought in wearing a stiff cushion cut from an old truck tire tied to her body with a cord around her waist. She could not walk; she could not even hobble. But she heard and believed my sermon about the Lord's servants' words being the same as the Lord's words. And when I said to her, "Go, according to your faith be it unto you," by faith she stood up, discarded the tire cushion, then walked, glorifying the Lord.

Shortly thereafter, one of our church members fell and cracked his skull open like a coconut, with each of the three cracks as wide as my little finger. After a violent attack of vomiting, he sank into a coma. For the next three days and nights, while the saints prayed, Chang and I also prayed for his healing, then carted him around in a handcart to three different hospitals. At each place the doctor's prognosis was the same–no hope for recovery. Desperate to help him, I finally bound his head tightly in a cloth and wheeled him home, where in Jesus' name I rebuked the demon distressing him. Immediately, he regained his senses and asked me where he had been and why I was there with him in his house. After I explained, I repented before him that I had waited so long, and asked for his forgiveness. Soon after, he recovered completely.

During that time, wherever I went, I was hounded by criticism that I dared to minister at all, especially by exercising authority in God's name over demons or diseases, without first being ordained. As crazy as I was to do only the Lord's work, and that mainly in tent crusades, soon my heart began to long to attend seminary and to be ordained.

A true source of encouragement to me at that time was Dr. Gjee Sun Kim, the "Elijah of the Orient," the "prophet of tears," who was also president of Dae Whan Theological (Interdenominational) Seminary in Seoul (which, sadly, has since become Taeshin College, a secular school). "Learn from me," he said. "Move your family up to Seoul, enroll as a student in my school, and lead a crusade on my campus. I will help you."

Believing that to be God's open door, I resigned the pastorate in Pibong, returned the military tent to the owner, and moved my family, including my mother and, of course, Chang and Lee to Seoul.

Dae Whan Seminary operated on the semester system, and special arrangements were made with the dean for me to enroll part-time at first, attending only one term of night classes per year.

Meanwhile, Chang, sturdy and citified, and I, underweight and sunburnt, continued to fulfill previous Evangelistic Healing Crusade Team commitments for the rest of the year in churches and meeting halls. We continued ministering together, laying hands on the sick, praying and seeing them restored to health, and dealing with demons, many of whom tried to argue with us. But we didn't argue; we simply commanded them to identify themselves, then cast them out in Jesus' name. These "normal" activities filled our everyday lives.

Eighteen

Flood

"Fear not, for I have redeemed you; I have summoned you by name; you are mine. When you pass through the waters, I will be with you; and when you pass through the rivers, they will not sweep over you." Isaiah 43:1c,2a NIV

1964–1967: Seoul, Samlae, Taegu

For two specific reasons I began supporting first one, then several struggling young seminary students by paying their tuition and living expenses: first, to encourage them to stay in seminary and study the Bible, thereby passing on the priceless encouragement I myself had received from Dr. Gjee Sun Kim; and second, because we needed their help with the tent during the Evangelistic Healing Crusade Team meetings.

Still not attending day classes, I was happy pitching the tent Kang Soon completed just before our May revival meetings, beating the drum, and preaching the Gospel. Tent evangelism was very expensive. Sometimes, but not always, people from the various villages helped out by serving us meals. But offerings from the tent meetings did not meet all our expenses. They were, however, subsequently covered by love offerings given for our ministry in churches, when it was too cold to meet outdoors in a tent.

In June 1964, Chang and I held our first meeting in Kang Soon's beautiful cotton tent at Samlae in south Choong Chun Province. We pitched it on the outskirts of town, then went out with the drum to advertise. Before the service, as I proclaimed my testimony in my very hoarse voice, and invited the people inside, God worked His miracles even outside the tent, dramatically healing a cripple and delivering him from his psychoses. As I went inside the tent, a charming child walked up to me and said that she had been lame all her life until just a few moments earlier, when the Lord God sovereignly healed her.

Just before the service began, an astonishing group of about thirty lepers came in and sat down just to the right of the pulpit. Some had their faces veiled, some sat with towels over their heads, and others wore linen gloves disguising their stubby fingers, all covering their deformities as well as possible. I shook hands with each of them, laid my hands on them, and prayed. With expressions of total surprise, each one testified right then and there that the dull heaviness that had stayed with them had simply left, and that all five senses had been restored to normal. It was amazing! One leper removed a hearing aid, claiming that, when I touched him, he heard thunder. To his surprise, he then discovered that his hearing aid was broken. Another, whose body had been tormented with itching, claimed to be completely freed from it.

While this was going on, the crowd backed away in horror. Most of them disappeared, not wanting me to touch them after I had touched the lepers. The few who stayed behind covered their heads with newspapers before letting me lay hands on them.

The following morning, all thirty lepers returned, each with a testimony of having been cleansed of his disease and completely healed overnight. One's face had actually been restored to its original appearance, and another's entire body was free from all the ugly spots. All during the next night, I wept for joy, meditating on the Word of God that comforted my heart:

> *But he was wounded for our transgressions, he was bruised for our iniquities: the chastisement of our peace was upon him; and with his stripes we are healed* (Isaiah 53:5).

From then on, the meetings, which usually lasted from 10:30 a.m. to 4 p.m., were so thrilling, I seldom took time for lunch.

In the spring of 1966, I finally enrolled as a day student at Myong-ji University, where I majored in Korean literature and language to earn a B.S. degree and to improve my public speaking.

I had begun my walk as a Christian within the Methodist denomination as a layman, then enrolled in the Presbyterian seminary to study for ordination, being no longer allowed to minister by the Methodists because I had baptized new believers by immersion. After studying awhile at that seminary, I discovered that the Presbyterian Church in Korea teaches a man-centered theology.

That August, I received ordination as an evangelist-pastor from World Mission (Assembly of God) by Jack Holm, an evangelist with the T.L. Osborn Association headquartered in Tulsa, Oklahoma, who had made contact with me earlier. Jack and I had ministered together quite successfully, traveling from one small rural village to another, in his new Mobile Evangelistic Unit (MEU), a four-door British LandRover station wagon, sent to him by his mission. In each village, where superstitions and ignorance abounded, we handed out simple Korean-language tracts, then played tapes and showed an Osborn Miracle Film powered by a generator.

Also during August, I approached the Korean Baptist Convention in Taejeon, and requested ordination from them as well. I wanted only to be God-centered in my thinking, and Bible-oriented in my Christian practice. So I began to search. When I learned that the ideal pattern of the Baptist denomination is the Early Church of the New Testament, I went to them with my request for ordination. Since I was already attending a seminary other than the Baptist Seminary in Taejeon, I was required to study further before they would ordain me to pastor one of their Baptist churches. So I studied.

In March 1967, Kang Soon herself entered Dae Hwan Seminary.

In July of that year, in Chilsung Market in Taegu, it took ten of us men to assemble Kang Soon's tent, erecting the posts and using one-and-a-half inch thick manila-hemp rope to secure the canvas to the frame and the concrete slab on which it sat—an unshakable, indestructible shelter, so we thought.

Since Jack Holm had graciously turned the MEU over to me when he left Korea, I sometimes parked it inside the tent, using the motor to run the generator to play the tapes and show the films.

That was the situation when one day, suddenly, for some inconceivable, arbitrary reason, I decided to skip praying for the people until the next day. "Why aren't you healing the sick?" someone asked me. "Why aren't you casting out the demons?"

"Because I decided not to!" I answered hotly, then turned away. As soon as I started to leave, a freak blast of wind slammed into the tent, rolling it around like a blanket. It loosened all the ropes, and incredibly bounced the whole concrete slab up into the air and back down. Stupefied, I could only stand and gape. When someone told me that Kang Soon and Sung Hyun were inside the tent, I raced in and found them stunned but safe, protected by a single metal post that had fallen down across the MEU parked near them.

Eternally grateful to God that they were unharmed, I wept and repented deeply before God, and prayed, "Forgive me, Lord. Give me spiritual sensitivity always. Let me always hear Your voice, obey Your word, and see the motions of Your hand."

By the time I entered into my fifth year of praying for a huge sturdy tent, Kang Soon's lightweight cotton tent was completely worn out. And the more I prayed for a really big tent, the clearer I could picture it in my mind, one that would accommodate 3,000 people safely and comfortably, but not too heavy or cumbersome for the Evangelistic Healing Team to transport from place to place. The design that eventually took shape in my imagination was so radically original that, even for me to remember all the details, I had to draw it exactly as I saw it in my mind. I wanted it constructed just like my drawing, and I visited thirty tent shops all over Seoul and Pusan, consulting with experts about making the tent.

Everywhere, the response was the same: No one could or would make and guarantee a 20-*pyung* (1350-square-yard) tent. Therefore, I decided to make it myself, estimating that I would need $3,000/US for materials. I knew the money was out there someplace; I just didn't know where or how to get it.

I needed help, so I advertised. I drew an architect's perspective to scale and, declaring my need for $3,000, submitted all the information to several foreign magazines, then eagerly watched the mail for the responses that never came. I then re-submitted it to *Faith Digest*. Right away, I received a ten-dollar donation as encouragement from Africa, then a few other small donations from other countries. I also received a response from international philanthropist, Dr. Len J. Johnson, President of the British Evangelical Society, whose travel plans to Japan included a brief side-trip to Korea on a certain Saturday. He agreed to meet with me to discuss my tent proposal if I could get to where he would be at the time.

During the packed week before the date of his visit, I led a revival-crusade on a mountain in the far countryside, while continuously reminding God in prayer that I had to end the meetings in time to be in that certain place at that specific time to meet Dr. Johnson during his very tight schedule.

All week long, it rained continually all day every day, all night every night. Torrents cascaded down through the rock crevasses and over the mountain walls. The mud thickened. Water-loosened rocks rolled and ricocheted down the mountainside.

While I preached the Word and prayed, I almost worried myself gray-headed about making the connection with Dr. Johnson. Friday night the meetings finally ended, and I lit out very early Saturday morning in the continual downpour. With a heavy pack strapped on my back and a big umbrella opened over my head, I urged my weary body to cover the seven-mile distance to the bus stop on the other side of the swollen river, in time to catch the one-and-only bus that would take me to Dr. Johnson.

Roaring waters converging at the narrow bend in the river had not only picked up speed, but had also raised the water level to a dangerous height, something I had not anticipated. The usual warning markers and even the wooden bridge across the river had been washed away. Still, the one thing on my mind was my meeting with Dr. Johnson to talk about the tent, and the words that came to my mind were, "the rivers, they will not sweep over you, will not sweep over you" (Is. 43:2 NIV).

As I reached the riverbank, the bus I had to catch came into view some distance away on the other side. I quickly hitched up my pants legs, stepped into the churning water that swirled up around my knees, and started wading.

I had gone only about twenty steps into the river when a voice behind me cried out, "Help! Please help me!" I looked back. A man, who had followed me down the hill into the river, was being swept downstream by the swift current. "Help me!" he yelled again. Then I saw him catch something and pull himself up onto the riverbank. No longer in danger, he hollered at me again, "How did you get that far into the river?"

I had been wading in water that was only knee-deep, and thought he might have stepped in a hole. So I pointed upstream and yelled back at him, "Over there is the right place. Come the way I came."

I sloshed further into the river, then looked back again. The man had moved up to where I had first stepped in, but the water level was then up around his chest. I did not understand why he was floundering in such shallow water unless the current had knocked him down, but I was sure he would be all right.

Gaining the opposite bank, I climbed up out of the water and boarded the waiting bus. When the driver noticed my pants legs rolled up and soaked to the knees, he said, "What did you do? You crossed the river? How was that possible? It's not possible!"

"It's possible," I said, while paying my fare. I looked back out the bus window and watched the other man still struggling to gain his footing in the shallows on the other side. When the bus moved on, I forgot about him, and concentrated my prayer on Dr. Johnson and the tent, thanking God that I was on the way and would arrive on time.

Dignified and clean-shaven, Dr. Johnson appeared to be about sixty years old, and struck me as a type of benevolent father, listening and responding with much interest and enthusiasm to my vision of the Big Tent. But his time in Korea was short, and he had to leave for Japan before he could make a firm decision about whether or not to support my project. A few months later, however, after having asked some probing questions about me, he returned to Korea from Japan, and we went together to a commercial bank where he simply signed a check for $3,000, and handed it over to me on the spot.

That is how God provided the money for the Big Tent.

Later on during the dry season, when I passed by that same bend in the river, I was amazed to learn that even at its lowest level, the river was still very deep and approximately 70 meters wide (230 feet). I said offhandedly to one of the locals, "Last year in the flood I walked through this river."

He scoffed. "Ha! Are you kidding? Since the creation of the universe, nobody has walked across this river in the flood."

Ah! I thought with renewed expectation, *if God was willing to help me walk through the flood like that, He must be planning to do marvelous things in that tent!*

Nineteen

The Big Tent

I will not venture to speak of anything except what Christ has accomplished through me in leading the Gentiles to obey God by what I have said and done–by the power of signs and miracles, through the power of the Spirit...I have fully proclaimed the gospel of Christ.

Romans 15:18,19 NIV

1967–1969: Seoul, Iri, Kang Kyong City, Seoul

Assembling and sewing the Big Tent–our collapsible, portable, canvas cathedral–proved to be a complicated, difficult process. It took 280 people working together for forty-five days to complete it, wearing out two heavy-duty, industrial Brother sewing machines, bending and breaking many needles in the process.

The money we spent on the tent equaled the cost of building a small church. But to me it was worth it. In my heart I wanted to hold only evangelistic tent-meetings throughout the rest of my life. The tent became my only workplace, a moving church, a soul-saving ship. In spite of how much I suffered from hunger and poverty while pitching tents, carrying them, and folding and unfolding the straw mats for the people to sit on, I loved the evangelical gatherings. Evidently the Lord loved them, too, because He kept demonstrating His miracle powers in tents just like He had in the Early Church, 2000 years ago.

In our growing experience, we discovered that sharing the Gospel with unbelievers, the chief aim of any evangelistic meeting, is severely undermined if unbelievers come to the services alone. Unfamiliar with church activities, they don't know what is going on. Unless Christians accompanied and supported them, it was too difficult for us to conduct dozens of evangelistic healing meetings productively. Unbelievers need tender guidance from believers, and that is why we always requested willing cooperation from the local churches. Also along with our volunteer student help, we always needed and asked the local Christians for help in pitching the Big Tent.

Surprisingly, in some places, when a local church council actively hindered us, some of their own ministers, who withdrew from them to take part in our work, proved to be as devoted to us as martyrs. In one city, where there were seventy churches, only one church cooperated with me. The leaders of the rest were determined not to allow their members to attend my revival meeting. We heard that on the streets and in the alleys they physically barred their members from coming. As they threatened further demonstrations against us, I considered canceling the meetings before we even began to advertise. Fearful of what they might do, I knelt down in an open field with my head on my knees. Without moving from that position for about four hours, I prayed aloud, complaining to God that our first meeting in the Big Tent would be impossible without His immediate help. Over and over I prayed, "Please, God, send people to the Big Tent and show Your miraculous signs!"

In spite of the threats, we pitched the tent at the edge of the city, set up our equipment, then advertised by marching up and down the streets beating the drum. Right up to the time to begin the service, only a few brave townspeople had shown up.

I went inside the tent and knelt down by the pulpit. Praying for God to bring the sick and the hurting of that town out to the meetings, I stayed on my creaky knees all through the opening songs and prayers, not even opening my eyes until time to stand up for the sermon. Meanwhile, they sang and prayed, sang and prayed, sang and prayed. Still I remained on my knees, praying to God, "Please, send people here to hear Your Word and receive healing from Your hand."

Finally, when I could stall no longer, I stood up and turned around. The place was packed–in front of me a sea of eager faces. Miracles were happening even before I opened my mouth to speak.

One miserable patient with a "leave of absence" from the Presbyterian "Jesus Hospital" nearby was healed as soon as he walked in under the tent flap. Two other men immediately and joyfully threw away their canes. Many who had been lame stood, then walked, then ran. A sixteen-year-old boy, blind and suicidal, gained his sight and with it his will to live. One man, whose hemorrhoids were so enlarged and putrefied that the stench was unbearable, was miraculously healed and completely delivered from his affliction.

Another man, almost dead from pneumonia, came up to me, coughing up bloody phlegm. I embraced him close to my side, with his face next to mine, and cried out for the Lord to heal him. Suddenly, he vomited right in my face. I subdued the nausea and revolting thoughts that assaulted my mind, while he continued coughing and vomiting. Soon, my entire face was covered, and his bloody sputum flowed into the side of my mouth as I continued to pray. But I kept on praying for grace until the nauseating thoughts invading my mind disappeared, until my mind focused on God's love and became peaceful. I knew then that God had done a work in him, so I released him, and proceeded to clean myself up before I preached my message.

Two months later, that same man attended another meeting I was holding. When he came up to me with a strong body, a healthy, shining face and clear eyes, I sank to my knees beside the pulpit and wept and praised God for His mercy, His love, and His healing power. From then on, anytime I thought of the sick as dirty, I quickly repented, willing to love them back to health.

By the next year, 1968, we were practically worn out, and so was the Big Tent. When it began to leak, we hauled it down to the riverside and waterproofed it by painting coal tar on the outside. But the ugly mottled-gray color made the tent look just plain dirty. Even worse, the tar coating made it much too hot inside. Since it was also very hard to find adequate space to set it up, we decided that in the winter season we would start making another tent like it, only smaller—one that would cover 960 square yards of space instead 1320, suitable for 2,000 people instead of 3,000.

Using big, salvaged strips torn from old, second-hand American military tents, Chang, Lee and I labored as a team to construct the new tent in a work area of only twenty-four square yards, using my very complicated drawing as a blueprint. With student volunteers from the theological seminary working together with us, it took 3,600 man-hours over a period of fifty days to make our big patchwork tent. When it was completed, we had no place to set it up to check it over until after we transported it south to the city of Iri, where we would conduct the next crusade.

In Iri, the most laborious, time-consuming part of the tent-raising was setting up the two iron center posts, each measuring 18 meters (approx. 54 feet high). When they were finally set, we assembled the rest, holding our breath not knowing what to expect. When it was finally up, we stood back to look. It was perfect! It was beautiful, like two pretty, light-brown patchwork umbrellas standing side by side. I thanked God with tears of joy for the miracles that surely would occur inside that miracle tent.

The beautiful tent was its own best propaganda, especially for attracting unbelievers, and it was crowded from the very first day of the crusade, when almost all who came were sick or lame. Immediately, people began to testify, crying out that their diseases had been healed. On the last day, no one in the gathering was suffering from disease. God had healed them all.

The same thing happened the following week in Kang Kyong City, miracles taking place from the very start. As the blind received their sight and the deaf their hearing, I saw my fifty-ninth known paralytic rise and walk, restored to health—Jesus Christ, the same yesterday, today, and forever!

Then came a mother and daughter, both suffering from crippling arthritis—the mother unable to move at all for four years! I reached my hands out to massage her hands, but before I even touched her, she whimpered and moaned and cried out in pain. I stood there, not knowing what to do until suddenly we were listening to the crackling sound of their joints breaking. She and her daughter were both completely healed.

A woman, deaf and mute for 36 years, heard and spoke. I praised God for this and for all the other miracles that happened in Kang Kyong City.

Caught up in the ministry throughout these crusades, I developed the habit of sleeping only four hours every night, seldom lying down before midnight, but always rising for early morning prayer, the custom of every Korean pastor.

Meanwhile, as I studied Baptist denominational policies, I made a very disheartening discovery: While proclaiming themselves to be Bible-centered, in practice the Korean Baptist churches were as fundamentally humanistic and legalistic as the Korean Presbyterian churches.

Sorely disappointed, I began to conceive the idea of someday starting my own full-Bible-believing denomination, which would use the Early Church of the New Testament as its ideal, where we could practice our faith through the power of the Holy Spirit.

The more I studied the Word of God, the more I saw that God's will is to give everybody freedom. People need to be taught that because of Jesus their sins are already forgiven. If the church does not preach that first of all, then people cannot be free because their sins remain. If they are not free, it is because they have not heard the true Gospel of forgiveness.

With that in mind, and somehow expecting my tent ministry to come to an end by 1970, on June 30, 1969, I took the first steps toward pioneering a new Baptist church in Seoul based on freedom of worship.

Twenty

Prayer: My Capital

Now faith is the substance of things hoped for, the evidence of things not seen. Hebrews 11:1

1969–1971: Seoul

I named the new church Youngdeung-po Baptist Church, which identified it with its geographical district in Seoul in the Shin Nahm area. Starting over once again with only myself, Lee, lay ministers Chang and Kim, Young-Kon, and seven other charter members, we held our first meeting in the Shin-Heung Building on November 30, 1969, in a third-floor rented room big enough for 200 people to sit comfortably on the floor.

The building was managed by a Buddhist, whose feisty, seventy-year-old father seemed determined to make life miserable for us. Every Sunday morning, he stationed himself in front of the entrance, where he kicked everybody coming in, even the women. He struck them with his fist, all the time heaping verbal abuse on them. He was not alone. The nearby Presbyterian and Methodist church leaders also displayed virulent hostility towards us by blocking the entrance while distributing handbills that defamed and slandered us, declaring that our Baptist beliefs were heresy.

In spite of their bitter antagonism, by our fifth month of meetings, the regular attendance topped 150 adult members, mostly former Presbyterians, all of whom I had rebaptized by immersion in Jesus' name (Acts 2:37,38; 19:5) as members of a Baptist congregation. Soon after, I took a second head count: 212 adult members had squeezed in with their 170 children, knee-to-knee, shoulder-to-shoulder on the floor. Encouraged by such numbers, we printed our first Sunday bulletin for the April 20, 1970, service.

In May, I replaced the traditional black curtain separating the ministers from the congregation with a yellow curtain, encouraged the men and women to sit together in families, and hired our first woman minister.

By June, I had completed the three-year evening seminary courses at Dae Whan Seminary. (It had taken me six years, one semester at a time.) I had also completed all the Korean language and literature courses at Myong-ji University, which I had begun in 1966.

In August, after more than eight months of continual harassment from the landlord and his father, we felt we had to move away from them. Fifty of our members stayed behind to maintain the work already started in that area, while the rest of us moved half-a-mile away to the third floor of another building in Youngdeung-po, and changed our name to Sung Rak ("Holy Joy") Baptist Church.

By the time my son, Sung Hyun, entered elementary school, I had moved my family from one rented room to another six times. Sung Hyun was beginning to show signs of strain. Still, he maintained his place as the top student in his class as well as class monitor. At that point, I was determined to buy property where we could build our own house and church building, and not have to move again.

I soon found what I wanted, what I believed God would provide for the new church site: a 350-pyong (12,600-square-foot) property for sale in Shinkil-dong, a muddy flood plain of the Han River–a dumping ground on the south side of Seoul, stinking badly and swarming with flies. Overcrowded, with no public transportation, no paved roads, no schools, no commercial area, with a reputation for burglaries, violent crimes, prostitution, and drunkenness, it was not a very proud parcel of land. It was also too big for a pioneer church the size of ours. But we were growing. I could almost see our future big, beautiful, clean church building and all the happy people coming and going and being blessed by God and the knowledge of His Word. At that time, however, our total weekly offerings averaged 20,000 won ($25/US); our yearly estimated budget, 1-million won ($1,250/US). The price of the land alone, 24-million won ($30,000/US), equaled our entire present church budget for the next twenty-five years.

Surveying the bogs and reeds, the piles of dung and the garbage heaps, I saw right away that we would need countless truckloads of clean dirt fill just to raise the elevation to where it needed to be. At the same time, I thought, *We have no money for this, but faith works like cash. That which is possible only needs a "Thank You, Lord." The impossible requires prayer, and prayer is my heritage as a Christian, my weapon against the impossible.*

Determined to have that property for the church, I began praying for it with all my might. I went to the location at least ten times and claimed out loud with certainty that God was promising me this land. I shouted to it, "Land, belong to me! Belong to me!"

Even though we had no money laid aside for this, and in spite of Korean law requiring any purchaser of land to pay the entire purchase price at the time of sale, I went to the owner with my offer to buy, and he laid down the conditions of payment, as follows:

Down payment–10 percent

Second payment within thirty days–40 percent

Third payment within the next thirty days–30 percent

Final payment within thirty days after the third payment–20 percent.

I thanked him, then went to the church and up onto the platform where I knelt before God all night and all the next day on sore, creaky knees, determined to have that land. Since prayer was my only capital, I needed to make some deposits in God's bank, so I prayed these same words over and over, "God, give the land to us! Give the land to us!" And I shouted through the walls and across the city to that miserable swamp in Shinkil-dong, "Land, belong to me! Belong to me!"

The next day, a few church members and I went and stood on the edge of the property, praising God and shouting dozens of times, "Land, belong to us!" Some of us shouted with all our might, but others murmured about the huge size and the foul condition of the property, and complained that it was surely impossible for us ever to buy it. I reminded them, however, that according to the Bible Jesus said:

"I tell you the truth, if anyone says to this mountain, 'Go, throw yourself into the sea,' and does not doubt in his heart but believes that what he says will happen, it will be done for him" (Mark 11:23 NIV).

"His promises were made for us," I said, "and this is not even a mountain. This is only a little flat piece of land. I believe with all my heart that God will give it to us." When they left, I stayed behind shouting at the property, "Belong to me!"

I prayed fervently while walking, riding the bus, sitting down, standing up. I never stopped. I prayed as if I were crazy, clenching my fists and focusing my entire strength on them, almost overwhelmed by fear that I would fail in prayer. Sometimes I became so ardent in prayer, I passed my destination, losing my way and direction. Once, to Kang Soon's great distress, I prayed for two-and-a-half hours while seated in front of the table without touching the fine meal she had prepared. But, how dare I, devoid of prayer, dream such a dream? I dared not!

When the contract was drawn up, the owner urged me to sign right then and pay him the full $3,000 down payment. But I had collected only 240,000 won ($300/US), which was only ten percent of what he was asking. When I did not sign, he angrily threatened to sell to someone else.

Desperate for the money, I tried every way I knew to get it short of stealing. Even as our members cut corners, made great sacrifices, and gave generously, none of them truly believed that the property would ever become ours. Engulfed by the doubts of others, I wept, lifting my petition up to heaven over and over, while searching for help on the earth.

I applied to the Korean-American Baptist Loan Committee for a ten-year construction loan to buy bricks for a temporary building on the site, negotiating with them for months, but they could do nothing for me without sufficient collateral. Suffering great inner anguish, I was finally able to negotiate a private loan at a very high interest rate. I used this money to buy security bonds on some other real estate—bonds I needed to offer the Loan Committee as collateral.

Once again, I visited the property owner, this time urging him to accept my $300 as earnest on the down payment, assuring him that I would bring him the balance of $2,700 by the end of the thirty-day grace period. We both knew that if I failed to do so, he could legally keep both land and money. He shrugged and agreed, so we signed the contract, and I went back to prayer. And I went back to begging and borrowing. Somehow I was able to pay off the rest of the down payment within the next two weeks.

Continually beside myself with anxiety, my heart ached within me, and my mind was in a total spin. Weeping before the Lord, I groaned and cried out to Him, "Lord, help me! Help me! How am I going to pay off the entire balance in ninety days? How am I going to pay off the second payment in the next thirty days?" I seemed to age 100 years, and either my clothes stretched or I shrank three sizes. The pain in my soul and my spirit was beyond description. One of my lay ministers came to me in tears, pleading, "Pastor, Pastor, let's give up!"

"No," I said, "we cannot give up. If we keep on praying to God, He will help us." And I labored in pain and in prayer day and night during that entire month until the second payment came due. I had visited everyone I knew and all their friends, begging to borrow the money, but there was no hope, no way to pay it as we entered the grace period for the second time.

On my way downtown on the bus, praying as usual, for some reason I got off in front of the main office of the Choheung Bank, and decided to try to get a loan from them. Guessing that the top executives had their offices on the top floor, I got in the elevator, closed the door, knelt down on the floor, and prayed with all my might, "Lord, help me meet the right executive! Help me meet..."

The elevator stopped at the eighth floor and the door quietly slid open. I stood up, dusted my knees, and stepped out, then followed the sign to the Auditor of the Headquarter Department. There I entered through their elegant, etched-glass doors, and asked the nearest secretary for an interview with the top auditor.

She led me into a cubicle and introduced me to the auditor, who asked me to sit down. I sat down, and then

I explained my situation to him. I said, "I am a servant of God. Please help me found a church. Help with God's work, and God will surely repay you for what you do for Him. I need to take out a loan."

He stared at me for a moment, asked me some questions, then laughed. "How naive you are," he said. "Pastor, no one in the world thinks like you do! Here," he said, shoving a printed sheet of paper towards me, "these are the twenty requirements for borrowing money from a bank, and you don't meet any one of them."

For two hours, I pleaded with him, reasoned with him, cajoled and pleaded some more, but without success. I finally left, but the next morning, after first praying from four o'clock until ten o'clock, I returned to his office. Very patiently, he explained everything all over again, then forcibly shoved me out the door.

Still believing that he was the one to give me the money, the next morning I prayed for another six hours, then visited him again. This time his secretary threw me out.

The fourth day, I wrote him the following letter, plus six more pages in the same vein, and I had it hand-delivered by a messenger:

Dear Sir,
God sent me to you. The Lord approached the fig tree and asked for figs even though it was not the time for

figs. The tree had leaves, but no fruit. From then on, that tree could not give fruit to anyone ever again. In the worldly view, according to what you said, it is impossible for me to get a loan from your bank. However, God sent me to you…

Two days later, I visited him again. As soon as he spotted me coming through his door, he scowled and growled at me, "Your letter was threatening! Who are you, that I should be threatened by the likes of you!"

So degraded in his eyes, I did not know what to say, so I began to pray. He became furious: "Stop that praying in here! This is not a church!"

Not knowing what else to do, I kept on praying, and I was thrown out again for the third time (on this my fourth visit). From then on, I began each day by praying for six hours about the situation, and every day after praying I visited him. They despised me; they disdained me; but I thought, *I don't care how strongly they feel against me. Someday I will die praying anyway.*

I visited him twenty-one times. On the day of my twenty-first visit, the down-payment grace period was up; all would be decided that day. According to my private-loan contracts, if I could not repay both my loans on that day, all that I had already paid would be forfeit, and I would lose both the land and the contract deposit. By that time, the stress of the situation had become so intolerably painful, I almost didn't care whether I lived or died. It was now or never: My creditors could do with me whatever they liked. I even invited them to meet me at the bank to get whatever it was they were going to do to me over with quickly.

In the elevator I once again knelt down on the floor and prayed, "Lord, a long time ago I gave myself to You, and You know all about this financial tangle I got us into. If I failed to do something right, I don't know what it is, so whether I live or die through the rest of this day is up to You. Whatever happens, I still believe in all the prayers I have ever made in Your name, and I will obey whatever You command."

Once again I got out on the eighth floor, this time fearing that all my efforts, all my dreams of a big church building and an expanding pastoral ministry had been in vain. I would soon know the worst. I stood before the door to the auditor's office afraid to go in, so afraid to face his secretary again, that I could feel my cheeks and ears flushing hot and red.

When the secretary opened the door, I stared. What happened to her? She was smiling. Then she said cheerfully, "The auditor is waiting for you."

I hurried into his office, wondering if I were going to my execution. But he first welcomed me, then asked his secretary to bring tea. I did not know how to act. The auditor chuckled and smiled, then shook his head and said, "Pastor, you are absolutely the most persistent and patient guy I have ever met in my life. Frankly, I'm afraid if I do not grant you the loan you are asking for, that God Himself will punish me. So, Pastor Kim, I have already taken care of your credit and everything. Go today to our branch bank in Namdaemoon. All the necessary paperwork is there ready for you, and you can pick up your check from them."

I burst into tears and buried my face in my hands. God had given me back my life. Within the next several minutes, all the overwhelming affairs with my creditors were resolved.

I went back to the church, collapsed on the platform in total exhaustion, and prayed myself away into a deep, deep sleep that lasted for almost two days. When I finally awoke, a church member said to me anxiously, "Pastor Kim, Pastor Kim, look at your face!"

I looked in the mirror and saw two white eyebrows arched over two sunken black eyes. I had prayed through such stress that my eyebrows had turned white.

Was it worth it? Of course! I already knew beyond any doubt that prayer moves God's heart. Prayer borrows God's hand. God waits for us to prevail in prayer, and helps those who are willing to abide in that place.

The battle, however, was still engaged, and would continue to be as long as I was determined to stand to the death in the breech between the stalking devil and those whom he sought to devour.

Twenty-One

Looking for Someone

"Every word of God is flawless; ...Do not add to his words, or he will rebuke you and prove you a liar. ...O Lord... Keep falsehood and lies far from me...." Proverbs 30:5-8a NIV

"Lord, to whom shall we go? You have the words of eternal life." John 6:68 NIV

1971–1978: Seoul

From the start of my new life with the Lord, I believed that God's original intention for His Word was that it be flawless and, consequently, not misleading; we are to obey it absolutely, and not blaspheme against Him with doubt. With this firmly planted in my heart and mind, back in April 1964, I discipled a young man, Hee-young Uh, whom I renamed Simon Uh after Simon Peter in the Bible. After him, I continued discipling and providing school expenses for two or three more people each year, mostly students from the Dae Whan Seminary, who became competent workers in the church. All of them received God's power to perform signs and miracles, served as members of the Evangelistic Healing Crusade Team, and eventually came to accept miraculous signs as the norm. After they realized that the key is simplicity, and learned to remain humble before the power, I helped many of them, including Lee, pioneer their own churches and serve in their own pastoral ministries.

And, because of the Evangelistic Healing Crusade Team's astounding success, I registered it, with the Korean government's sanction, as a California USA-based ministry.

In 1971, after we had finally gained possession of the Shinkil-dong property, we built a small brick sanctuary. With no symbolic cross that might distract new members' attention away from Jesus and the teachings of the Bible, we held our first service on November 30, soon increasing to two Sunday services.

By early 1972, 170 families of our church membership had built their homes on the church property, an area where the shoe-shiners and taxi drivers refused to come during the muddy, rainy season. To convince first-timers to attend our services, some of our church members even offered to clean their shoes and wash their clothes after they returned home.

By then, it had been over five years since I first requested ordination from the Korea Baptist Convention

(August 1966) in Taejon. Baptist pastors in Korea at that time came in three categories: 1) not graduates of any seminary; 2) graduates of the Baptist seminary; or 3) graduates of other seminaries. Since I qualified in the undesirable category three, my request had been followed by five frustrating years of questions:

1. "Do you speak in tongues?"

"Yes." Speaking in tongues, however, was not a "Baptist thing," and my response resulted in many, lengthy assignments for the next few years to research the subject, along with persecution probably intended to discourage me from my stand that tongues are for today.

2. "Do you believe in and practice miraculous healing?"

"Yes." They gave me more research assignments, more persecution for the same reasons.

3. "Do you believe in and practice casting out demons?"

"Yes." They assigned even more extensive research, followed this time by more intense persecution not only against me, but mockery and insinuations targeting my church members as well. This harassment against them resulted in some of them leaving the church.

In March 1972, I finally completed all the Taejon Baptist School's preliminaries, including the oral interview by the Baptist examiners. It's a miracle they ordained me at all.

Then, on August 18 that year, the flood came without mercy upon the entire Youngdeung-po area, which included our land in Shinkil-dong. Soon, all that could be seen of our brick building above the water was part of the roof. Two persons, a lay minister and a guard, who had broken a hole through the roof, crawled out and stood on the top calling for help. They were rescued by the Regional Reserve Forces. All 170 houses on our property were inundated by the filthy floodwaters. Everything the families owned was destroyed.

As a result, many of our remaining church members, along with much of the local population, moved to safer ground in the city, and our membership fell dramatically. Government officials cordoned off the area as a "flood district," and we had to hold worship services in an alley near the elementary school until after the flood waters abated. Even then, swarms of disease-bearing flies covered the area, and for months we were unable to obtain a permit to rebuild.

When the land finally became dry, we cleaned the church building as well as we could and began worshiping there once again on November 23, 1972. But the battle was far from over: Soon thereafter, fires destroyed the neighboring slums. When about 300 of our near neighbors were suddenly homeless, I made a refuge for them in our church with food and blankets and fuel for three months until they could get relocated. Many of the remaining Sung Rak families lost their homes to the fires, and they also moved away, some never to return.

Before all this happened, I had been trying to expose my impressionable son to the excitement and thrill of seeing God move in revival meetings, and I could only wonder what he was gaining from the sum and substance of all these disasters.

The foundation of trusting in God and His Word proved secure in the few remaining faithful students and church members; these all acknowledged that believing the Bible absolutely had changed their lives completely by enabling them to perform miracle signs with great power. These future leaders started their own Saturday morning Bible study groups to encourage others to emulate, as they did, the Bereans in the Bible:

> *Now the Bereans...received the message with great eagerness and examined the Scriptures every day to see if what Paul said was true* (Acts 17:11 NIV).

The primary aim of all the study groups was the same, to search the Scriptures daily to learn all about the God of the Bible. As the little groups studied only the Bible and learned to love Jesus and the Word, they brought their lives more and more under the authority of the Bible, thereby becoming more like the Lord Himself. To ensure that each person received the same amount and quality of attention, discipling, and encouragement as the others, the Saturday groups patterned themselves more-or-less after the Methodist "Circle Bible Study" and the Presbyterian "Class Meeting," thus limiting attendance to only a few in each group, and thereby multiplying the number of small groups. At the same time, several seminary students asked me to meet with them as their teacher; our group alone was unlimited in the number allowed to attend.

Soon, we all began referring to ourselves informally as "Bereans," acknowledging three fundamental precepts: Bereans do not quarrel; they are humble, teachable before the Word; and they establish their faith firmly by meditating deeply on the Scriptures.

The study groups soon became very popular, especially since "demonstration of the Spirit's power" (1 Cor. 2:4 NIV) was an extension of the primary aim. As a result, church membership quickly shot up again to about 400. But the flood and the fires had made our poor even poorer, and despite three Sunday services, offerings were so meager that, by the end of 1975, Sung Rak's estimated total worth came to only $2,500. Regardless, it was time to rebuild, even though we knew that amount was only enough to scratch the surface of the ruin and rubble.

Twenty-Two

The Church Alive

...the just shall live by his faith.

Habakkuk 2:4; also Romans 1:17;
Galatians 3:11; Hebrews 10:38

1975–1994: Seoul

Once again, we gathered bricks and blocks and began construction, this time on our second sanctuary. I often worked alone while my church members rebuilt their own homes, with the military government watching us. We were asked to report to them what I preached in our services, where our occasional foreign-guest speakers came from, what time they preached, and how many people attended. Whenever I accompanied foreigners to local areas, the police stopped us, asked for identification, and questioned our purpose and activities. It soon became extremely burdensome.

The entire nation was under curfew from midnight to 4 a.m., but that had a bright side: The city often sent workers during those hours to clean up the streets and roads.

By then, my association with the Korean Baptist Convention and their influence over our congregation had become quite disheartening, to say the least. Not only that, but so many members had left the original Sung Rak Baptist Church during that time, I realized it was time for me to get serious about pioneering a full-Bible-believing denomination, on my heart since before 1970—one where we could obey the Bible in all things, seeking the operation of God's supernatural gifts through the Holy Spirit.

As a congregation, we had taken two giant steps forward: One, we had moved into our second church building which was completed after four years of construction; and two, the Saturday Bible study groups consolidated as Berea Academy, and soon became the empowering core of Sung Rak Baptist Church.

In 1981, Deacon Chang left us and pioneered his own ministry, Seoul Life Baptist Church, where he successfully practices what he learned during those years working with me and while studying at Berea Academy.

In January 1982, consciously aware at all times that faithfulness to God is the source of church growth, I began planning our present sanctuary by studying church architecture to decide what kind of building would best reflect all that Sung Rak stood for. Many church buildings–memorial cathedrals with mystery and history, which they can trace back to the Tabernacle in the Old Testament–need pillars to support some shape on the outside. Unfortunately, that structure often promotes the same fear as does the inside of dark and dreary gothic buildings.

For us, the old traditional architecture was unsuitable. I reasoned this way: *Jesus comes into each believer, so Christian churches should be operated around the congregation, not the sanctuary. The Word became flesh, so wherever He goes–to the waterfront, to the desert, to the market, to the mountainside–there is the congregation. Therefore, when people enter a New Testament church operating around the congregation, they should feel like they could be at the waterfront, the desert, the market, the mountainside–all together as one.*

Keeping that in mind, I designed the building trying to eliminate all obstacles that kept the people inside separated from the people outside, and to make the sanctuary as big and open as possible by placing certain structures–elevators, for example–outside.

Instead of pledging to a building fund, our people dedicate their lives, their work, their offerings, and all our church services to God. They give to God, not to a building. Many of them don't even know what the money will be used for until the building is built. I don't talk about money—I only teach them God's Word.

By January 1988, I had read the Bible through 108 times since the fall of 1957, and supported 32 seminary students since 1965, including fourteen members of my own family and eighteen strangers.

In September of that year, my mother died. She had learned to read in church, singing the lyrics to our hymn-songs written out in *hangul* (Korean alphabet) on posters in the front of the sanctuary. She loved the Lord her God with all her heart, mind, soul, and strength, and had spent most of her waking hours reading the Bible and praying, frequently starting at 4 a.m. and continuing almost all day every day until her death.

In 1988, we incorporated the South Baptist Convention of Korea with 160 member churches. In 1990, we broke ground for our third sanctuary with 6,500 seats. In 1991, an article about the Big Tent appeared on page 306 of the *Guinness Book of Records*. By June 1992, Sung Rak Church had 67,214 adults enrolled in membership, plus their children (by January 1996, over 80,000 adults).

It is not wealth, but ideas that contribute to the people's well-being. As long as we keep thinking ahead, not being idle, but always wondering what could improve the lives of others, we will continue coming up with new ideas.

In the fall of 1992, I received a letter from a clergyman in New Jersey challenging me about the first woman I raised from the dead in 1962 in Kwang-si. He doubted that it was true, and said that the person should appear before people and testify to the event.

All I remembered about her was that she attended the Kwang-si Baptist Church, nothing more, and I had had no contact with her at all since that time. But the week after I got his letter, while I was teaching a very crowded class at the Berea Academy, a woman I did not recognize came up to the podium at break time and introduced herself to me: "I am Deaconess Noh Je Sook, that lady your students were just talking about. Not only am I still alive, but since then, I am mother again and grandmother."

Unfortunately, the clergyman in New Jersey was killed in a car wreck before he heard of her testimony. We pray he will meet her in heaven.

In March 1993, the principal of Imsung Middle School in Yesan established the "Kim, Ki Dong Corner" in the school hall at the top of the stairs. Along with the history of the school itself, several copies each of the 120 books I had already written are displayed on a bookshelf, available to the students. (In each one the reader gets a strong dose of the Gospel.) On the opposite wall hangs my photograph as a role model–their ancestor-student, one very poor Korean, who overcame abject poverty to become a well-known teacher and preacher in Korea and other countries as well.

Epilogue: Worthless Servant

Oh, the depth of the riches of the wisdom and knowledge of God! How unsearchable his judgments, and his paths beyond tracing out! "Who has known the mind of the Lord? Or who has been his counselor?" "Who has ever given to God, that God should repay him?" For from him and through him and to him are all things. To him be the glory forever! Amen.

Romans 11:33-36 NIV

Very early in my walk with the Lord, I realized that the great duties of my life on earth are to evangelize the lost, heal the sick, deliver the demon-possessed, teach His Word, and pastor His church–the optimal, non-negotiable conditions upon which my life depends. Those are my duties, but prayer is my joy.

Prayer is my capital. Just as any successful building project requires a continual flow of sufficient and timely capital, so any powerful, lasting ministry requires a continual flow of travailing and prevailing prayer. Although vital to evangelizing, prayer is even more vital to pastoring God's people, discipling them to grow in spirituality and reach higher dimensions in their spiritual lives.

Evangelism is like scattering seed. Pastoring is like parenting a multitude of children through puberty and adolescence into mature, responsible, and productive adulthood. A successful pastoral ministry is not easily achieved.

Evangelism and pastoral ministry are both precious in the Lord's eyes, but making disciples is the Lord's specific assignment for His Church–saving souls, but also saving lives. Jesus said:

> "*Therefore go and make disciples of all nations, baptizing them in the name of the Father and of the Son and of the Holy Spirit, and teaching them to obey everything I have commanded you. And surely I am with you always, to the very end of the age*" (Matthew 28:19,20 NIV).

I recognize that God gave me special gifts. At the same time, I know I have the duty to share all that I discover about God in relation to His Word without hoarding it to myself. This is because it is experiential phenomena rather than rules and doctrines that cause His Church to grow.

I have been and remain totally opposed to ecclesiastical authority and secularism within the Church, determined to dedicate myself to upholding only the truth of the Gospel based on the New Testament. Our church is committed to protecting our rights to freedom of faith, freedom of biblical interpretation, and freedom of theology because the Bible says that the Holy Spirit Himself teaches us (1 Jn. 2:27).

Back in 1964, having read through the entire Bible seventy-five times, I saw the panorama of the entire Bible as one picture. Still, I had numerous questions, always wondering why the Bible included many questionable events. In spite of my questions, I tried not to doubt. I believed and spoke positively as I read, blindly accepting the Bible's simple spiritual consciousness as God's intention that there be no mistakes in the Bible, and that we do not add to it or take away from it (Rev. 22:18,19), lest we come into error. Therefore, I judge the attitude of those who ask doubtful questions without seeking true answers to be blasphemy.

What the Bereans wanted to know, I also wanted to know. By reading the contents of the Bible through dozens of times, one by one my questions found solutions. Realizing that, I began filling my mind with God's infinite words, and His words in turn have become my inspiration. I call that "discovering God's intention." In any given situation, as soon as I recognize

God's intention, I feel power surge in my body, and I act on it; consequently, signs and miracles still happen through me today.

When I first began leading revival meetings as an evangelist, spreading the Gospel and healing the sick, several older ministers and believers encouraged me. Others gave me warning, that a number of other workers had also performed signs and miracles in the past, but continued for only a few years. At first, I believed the works of those others to be proof of true ministry, but I was mistaken for several reasons that are explained in the Bible:

First, their flow of supernatural power was disrupted because they did not continue to pray for it:

> *Then came the disciples to Jesus apart, and said, Why could not we cast him out? And Jesus said unto them, Because of your unbelief.... Howbeit this kind goeth not out but by prayer...* (Matthew 17:19-21).

Second, they did not know the Bible:

> "*God is not a man, that he should lie, nor a son of man, that he should change his mind. Does he speak and then not act? Does he promise and not fulfill?*" (Numbers 23:19 NIV)

> "*For nothing is impossible with God*" (Luke 1:37 NIV).

Third, they did not have faith:

"*...Everything is possible for him who believes*" (Mark 9:23 NIV).

Jesus Christ is the same yesterday and today and forever (Hebrews 13:8 NIV).

I was determined to balance these three precepts—prayer, knowledge, and faith—and to put them into practice. However much others in the past acted in unbelief, I believed and obeyed God's Word at any rate. And the Lord's power has been working in me for the past three and a half decades.

Now, I teach others how to understand the Bible, how to believe it, and how to obey it by accepting every word as truth. I believe that the more we know, rely on, and obey the Bible, the more promises of the Bible we will experience, and the more we will discover God's intention in any situation, and how to give Him opportunities to help us.

I believe that the apathy and agony of modern churches lie in their lack of apostolic power, and that the casting out of evil spirits, one of the Lord's commands to us (Mt. 10:7,8), is only a matter of using that readily available power.

I teach others to use the intercession described in the Gospels and the Epistles to perform the same signs performed in the Early Church.

I believe that churches who lose their zeal for missions are dying churches: Missionaries go into other places as living bombs. Bombs explode, sending pieces in every direction; therefore, we should not be afraid of dying on foreign soil.

I consider prayer our greatest blessing, our greatest heritage from the Lord. I believe that the Holy Spirit does not reveal Himself to those who restrain Him by doubting or by neglecting prayer. The only reason I know how to pray and to grasp the power of prayer is simple and basic: I read and believe the Bible.

I also believe that I author my own personality; it is my masterpiece. Still, shyness is my main weakness, but my will can overcome most of the other weaknesses of my personality.

Faith comes from keeping my promises to God; confidence comes from within myself; credibility comes from other people.

I believe that revival is here, and that God is looking for someone with faith, confidence and credibility—someone who is after His heart.

In spite of my earnest desire to serve only the Lord, there are times in my life when I sin. But as soon as I realize I have done something—anything—to displease Him, I repent immediately, and ask Him to forgive me, then I go on. I do not live in the pit of regret.

With deep appreciation I know that if my wife, Kang Soon, a beautiful woman of prayer, had not married me, I would be in a totally hopeless situation today. She is a most humble person, better than I.

I need not have concerned myself about Sung Hyun's reaction to all the disasters that came against us. He maintained an excellent record at Seoul University, applying himself to the study of English and Psychology, then mastered the one-year prerequisite entrance courses for Oxford Manchester Theology Seminary, where he now prepares himself for eventually undergirding the Sung Rak Church.

Meanwhile, the Holy Spirit constrains me each week to list my sins and shortcomings of the week on the back of Sung Rak's Sunday bulletins, to expose myself to the congregation as merely one of them, and to turn their gaze upon the Lord Jesus Christ, Who alone is worthy of their honor and praise.

What are we of the Sung Rak Baptist Church hoping for? We hope to live our lives according to God's intention, then stand without shame before Jesus Christ our Lord when He comes again. We hope to receive His compliments; but even then, it will be quite proper for us to bow down and confess to the King of Glory, "I am Your worthless servant, Lord."

NAKED AND NOT ASHAMED
by T.D. Jakes.
With a powerful anointing, Bishop T.D. Jakes challenges us to go below the surface and become completely and honestly vulnerable before God and man. In relationships, in prayer, in ministry—we need to be willing to be open and transparent. Why do we fear? God already knows us, but He cannot heal our hidden hurts unless we expose them to Him. Only then can we be *Naked and Not Ashamed*!
TPB-156p. ISBN 1-56043-835-5
(6" X 9") Retail $11.99
Also available as a workbook.
TPB-56p. ISBN 1-56043-259-4
(8 1/2" X 11") Retail $6.99

Available at your local Christian bookstore

See all our exciting books on the Internet!
http://www.reapernet.com